WHAT OTHERS ARE SAYING
ABOUT THIS BOOK

"*The Goodness Experience* gives you the tools to having a Better more fulfilling life in order to become the Best version of the grandest vision of YOU possible."
— Darlene Headley, Executive Assistant, Teachers Health Trust

"The Goodness Experience addresses a complex part of women's lives. Janice's passion and determination to empower all women to love themselves and own their personal beauty is apparent in every chapter of this heartfelt book. The 'Nag' (love the name) lives within all of us, seemingly to ruin our experiences. Janice has given us new power and a method that works for dealing with that nasty voice in our heads ... love it."
— Kate McDowell, Real Estate Agent, Sotheby's International

"The powerful message in the words of *The Goodness Experiences* saved my sanity. This book gave me such insightful and easy tools to use that it profoundly changed my life."
— Wendy Dearborne, President, Adassa James Institute Inc.

"An easy read packed with potent messages that will transform your experience of love, contentment and happiness. A huge contribution to the quality of my relationships and life. If the Nag takes over, I now know that I have a choice to listen to her ... or NOT! I have the tools to experience abundance and love in my life and to kick out the victim. Thank you! Thank you! Thank you."
— Claire Roth, Principal, Roth Enterprises, Inc.

"Janice Marie has written a fun book ... tauntingly honest, deliciously funny, and profoundly important."
— Ron J. Hennessey MS., Assistant Director, Associated Counselors of Southern Nevada

The Goodness Experience

A Life in Harmony

Janice Marie M.A.

THE GOODNESS EXPERIENCE Publishing

The Goodness Experience: A Life in Harmony

by Janice Marie

Copyright © 2006 Janice Marie Wilson / Jann Robbins
ISBN-10: 0-9653077-1-9
ISBN-13: 978-0-9653077-1-0
First Edition: August 2006

Published by:
THE GOODNESS EXPERIENCE Publishing

Phone: 702-233-8305

Website: www.thegoodnessexperience.com

The authors and publishers of this book do not dispense medical advice or prescribe any technique as a form of treatment for physical or emotional problems and therefore assume no responsibility for your actions. The intent of this material is to provide general information to help your quest for emotional and spiritual growth. We encourage you to seek professional assistance for all areas of healing.

Printed in the United States of America

Table of Contents

ACKNOWLEDGEMENTS

Thank you to everyone who has made *THE GOODNESS EXPERIENCE* a reality.

Carolyn Proctor for her expert eye and editing skills.

The beautiful cover design and unique illustrations by Kroutil Artists, LTD.

Tony Stubbs, publishing consultant for his hard work in transforming the manuscript into this beautiful book.

Jann Robbins, my editor for her unceasing dedication, relentless pursuit of excellence and friendship.

My family, who supported me through every step of this project and taught me so many lessons and continue to fill my life with goodness experiences ... every day in every way.

INTRODUCTION

The day we were born, there was a promise of hope for each of us to have a life of happiness, perfection, fulfillment, and intelligence. Everything good that one could desire was held in that spiritual promise. Not one of us was left out. At least that's what our mothers told us, but boy, were they wrong! What were they thinking?

We grew up hoping we could do it all, have it all, be it all. *But,* the real world challenged that rainbow-hued promise. What had changed? Why did we hit stumbling blocks? When did everything start falling apart?

Each of us has hit a 'wall' at one time or another and scrambled for answers. We scream and cry and ask, "Why me? Why did this happen? How can I get my life back on track?" Or, sometimes we just sweep it under the rug and leave it for another time. We're left floundering and wondering if there is any good left in the world.

Later in life, after a few failures, we cling to the advice and approval of others. We hope they will show us the way. Those 'others' may say, "No matter where you've been, what you've been through, what you have, or what you don't have, that promise, the one we were given when we were born, is still the truth about life." What a relief; we're off the hook. Everything will be okay someday. But, somehow and someway, *someday* never comes.

I didn't believe any of those words of advice when my world came crashing down around me. I had to pick up the pieces and look for a way to experience what I wanted in *my* life; not someday, but now. I was tired of being disappointed and frustrated, and desperately needed answers. I prayed, I hoped, I pleaded with whatever powers were in control, but I was still floundering and lost. I tried to find answers from other people. "Help me," was my continuous quest. I blamed God; why wouldn't He help me from all the problems that had culminated in my life?

I thought about others I knew and admired; they didn't seem to be falling apart. I knew they had similar challenges. Why could they overcome their problems while I couldn't?

One morning when I couldn't take any more confusion, despair, or anxiety, I went to the mirror and looked at myself. I had fallen into a trap of over-analyzing, over-scrutinizing, and over-angst-ing about everything. I was mentally drained and knew there had to be a better way. This was the day I began my journey to learn how to live my life more fully, love more deeply and laugh more freely.

This was the beginning of my Goodness Experience. I didn't find all of my answers instantaneously, but I knew in my heart I was on the right path. I had made a conscious decision to experience *only* a fulfilling, positive reality; I wasn't going to quit until I lived my life with a wonderful sense of *abandon, optimism* and *expectation* of Good. I was going to reach the end of the rainbow.

Sounds too good to be true, doesn't it? Pollyanna in attitude. Naive? Not at all. It is reality. And it *is* true for each and every one of us.

From practicing the Goodness Experience, I have discovered there are perfect answers for every problem. There is a foundation of truth and love that we all have. When we understand how these Laws of Goodness work for us and when we acknowledge our Divine Connection whose source is in God, Goodness, we find freedom. Regardless of what religion you subscribe to or what beliefs you hold, there is a Goodness principle that provides you with every answer you need for a life of fulfillment.

If this is a freedom you yearn for, read on.

This book was designed to be your personal journey, a return to your natural Goodness inside. The note pages at the end of the chapters are a place to journal. Use them any way you choose. See what happens when your true heart is congruent with love and goodness.

CHAPTER 1

WHEN IT ALL BEGAN

When I was growing up, I had dreams and hopes, typical girlhood fantasies. Fairy tales, sugar and spice and everything nice, a handsome prince charming, a castle and a life of 'happily ever after.' You probably had those dreams, too, filled with hope.

When I fell in love the first time, I was three years old. My mother took me to the ballet, and it was true love as I watched the graceful fairy princess float across the stage and passionately leap into the arms of Prince Charming. The costumes were breathtaking to my young eyes, and the music touched my heart as never before. The stage, the scenery, and the lights captivated my imagination. I was in another world, where every life on stage had a happy ending. I believed that ballerinas were surely angels. The beauty and grace of their movements inspired me.

From that day on, I lived to become a ballerina. This was my first dream of what I wanted from life. It also became my first disappointment and it was a big one. I had short legs and a hard time remembering my left from my right. Not exactly prima ballerina material.

By the time I was ten, I remember my teacher looking at me as though I were a fireplug, and not too bright, to boot. When I wasn't chosen to be in the diva circle of little girls who were leggy, lithe, graceful and ready for the stage in the first recital, I cried all night. My mother dried my tears and I became determined I wasn't going to give up. I remember lying in my bed at night, wondering how I could possibly reach my destiny as prima ballerina on a New York stage. Each morning, my determination to achieve was stronger.

Undaunted, I begged my mother for private lessons. I was sure I could overcome my shortcomings and was determined to work hard because I knew in my heart that being a ballerina was my destiny.

My mother explained private lessons were expensive and we couldn't afford it. Oops! Not only were my legs too short and I didn't know my right from my left, but now I wasn't rich enough to achieve my dreams. Life was a disaster and I felt the world was against me.

I trudged through a few more years trying to overcome my mechanical difficulties. However, my love for ballet never lessened, yet, my frustration grew. Little did I realize this was only the beginning of an unyielding NAG-i-tive voice that I would later nickname the NAG.

And then it happened! When I was twelve, my mother found an incredible ballet teacher named Kate. She had just arrived in my town from New York City and was looking for students. In order to afford the lessons, my mother took an extra job and surprised me with the gift I longed for – semi-private lessons with a real live prima ballerina.

The first day I went to class, my mother drove me to the wealthiest part of town during her lunch hour. I was anxious as I sat next to her. After we'd pulled up in front of a three-story mansion, my mother and I walked up the sidewalk excitedly and rang the doorbell. The man who answered instructed us to wait in the foyer. I looked up toward a sweeping staircase and saw a tall, thin woman standing on the landing, a beautiful ballerina in a lavender leotard and tutu. As she came down the stairway, she appeared to be floating – the *most* graceful and beautiful image I had ever seen. I am sure my mouth dropped open. I felt myself trying to stretch to make myself tall and thin like this ballerina.

Kate changed my life. She didn't see short legs but instead a girl who loved the art of dancing, and helped me overcome my hesitation between 'left and right.' My mother's sacrifice had somehow given me confidence, and Kate saw my heart's desire. Her smile of approval made me believe I was the ballerina I'd always dreamed of being.

Later, I danced professionally for twelve years in musical comedies, summer theatres, with the Gus Giordano Company in Chicago, and toured with a nightclub act around the world. I also taught ballet and jazz, helping others to achieve their dreams.

In retrospect, this was my first Goodness Experience. I realize now the importance of this event was not in 'getting what I wanted,' but in *giving what I wanted.'* I was *giving* my heart and soul to my desire to be a ballerina. When I made this change in my thinking, I began seeing myself in a new way. I was living my Goodness Experience by living and giving from the heart and feeling love, seeing love, and expressing love. This total commitment made my desires a true and distinct reality.

Now, even though this was not an earth-shattering circumstance, it was earth-shattering in my understanding, and taught me that my desires can become real when I listen to my heart instead of buying into the opinions of others, or into my own doubting thoughts. I was convinced in my heart I was a beautiful ballerina and, once I felt that conviction, nothing could stop me. Through my motive of giving love, feeling love and experiencing love through dance, I was free to accomplish my goal.

Later, as a teenager and into my adult life, I faced many of life's rejections and disappointments, as we all do, and found believing in my heart's desire more difficult. My doubt and fear were overwhelming, my conviction wavering. I became confused, and constantly questioned and doubted myself. This confusion led to floundering and I became more insecure by the moment. It seemed easier to listen to others' opinions of me and depend on their advice. At this point in my life, I was sure they knew more than me; also this *justified and released me from any responsibility.* I blamed everyone for my failures. 'They' always explained that, for one reason or another, over which I had no control, I was inadequate. That was just the way it was, and it wasn't my fault.

How could I be expected to achieve with so many inadequacies? I didn't realize at the time I was buying a picture that wasn't true. I felt justified in accepting myself as inadequate. I had reached an impasse at this point.

My failures were not just a single event that caused me to question my value, but an accumulation of events that had bombarded my life. This is when the pain began. Isn't that the way it always begins? One failure on top of another and another? Like a cascading waterfall of NAG-i-tivity! So in my insecurity, I tried to protect myself from more emotional pain by feeling absolutely nothing. I was afraid to trust my heart's desire; if I had a heartfelt desire, I stifled it because I knew it would never work out.

I didn't understand at the time, but later realized, this gap between despair and fulfillment is created when we're not listening to our **Divine Connection** and not following our heart. The result of not listening to the voice of Goodness had created a nightmare for me.

I was listening to fear every day. It was a voice that had overtaken my entire life and it was NAG-i-tive, demanding and angry. There was always a NAG-ging sense of failure about the future. I was anxiety-ridden, and tried to medicate my problems away, but that didn't work.

My story is not unusual; this is something we all battle with, usually daily. I was not unique in my dilemma. Everyone has their own set of doubts and fears, the same kind of hurt feelings and unmet desires, even though the circumstances may be different.

I'm sure you recognize the voice of NAG-i-tivity I heard – the voice that says, "You're too fat," "You're too poor," "No one will ever love you," "You're not pretty," and, "You're not even smart." What happened to the old adage, "If you don't have brains, you'll have looks and vice versa"?

My world was a disaster. Between the moment I opened my eyes in the morning to the end of the day, I was so frustrated I could hardly do anything but go through the motions of living. I did what I set out to do. I became numb on the outside, but inside I felt angry and bitter. Well, what else could I expect? Garbage in – garbage out. I was absorbing all the NAG-i-tive thoughts that were racing through my mind.

This continual battle seemed non-stop. I was looking for approval from others, working tirelessly to show them how perfect I was. But at night when I lay my head on the pillow and mentally went through the day, I focused on what I'd done wrong, and how I'd failed. I tossed and turned with anxiety, agonizing over how I could possibly straighten out my world. Would I ever find happiness and feel good about being alive? I knew there had to be something more, a better way of living. My life was clearly spinning out of control, with only stolen moments of contentment. I dreaded tomorrow and I felt empty and hopeless today.

How Did I Look at Things?

When I was asked the age-old question, "Is your glass half-empty or half-full?" I felt that neither was a good answer. Why can't it be full and overflowing? I wanted everything! Did that make me self-absorbed, self-centered or selfish? I didn't think so because I wanted it for everyone, not just me. But, then again, did I want everything good, or was my ego demanding I *be* everything? That I *be* the center of attention at all times?

It seemed my whole life had been a search to find this overflowing Goodness that I always believed possible ...

BUT ...

There's always that B-word. "Yes, I believe it's possible ... *BUT!* That tiny word is the killer of so many right desires. Those three letters have diminished hope, happiness and abundance unwittingly for thousands throughout the centuries.

How I wish I'd never known that word. After meeting a dead end to all my hopes and desires, pausing, hesitating, fearing, halting, sitting in the discontentment of unfulfilled dreams, I decided I needed answers. Realizing my heart's desire became my purpose – living in the fulfillment that my heart yearned for each day, not just "wishing" it so. I decided I couldn't settle for less.

That's when I learned I didn't have to *be* everything to experience all the Goodness in the world. What a relief! I needed to magnify the Goodness I already possessed. I had to learn to *activate*, *allow* and *accept*. This continuing flow of Goodness was the *promise* given to me the day I was born.

Activate, Allow, Accept

An experience of only Goodness in your life is no fantasy. It is reality, a truth that comes naturally from loving and valuing yourself and the world around you. It is the Universal Law of Life that supports each of us.

In the following pages, you will be asked to spend time living to *activate* your Goodness Experience; discovering your ability to *allow* Good to come to you, and realizing your ability to *accept* an overflowing glass that is filled with abundance, enabling you to give freely to yourself and those around you.

Activating, allowing and *accepting* opened the door to a life in harmony. I found the only obstacle was *me*, and the limitations I unwittingly imposed. It was that voice of doom. I had no idea where it came from, but I began to recognize it as:

THE NAG!

Please turn the page and meet your NAG ...

"Hi, nice to meet you. My name is
NAG. I'm your best friend. I'm a
drama queen, a spoiled brat, a
sore loser. I'm a tangled mess of
emotions ... just like you. How do
you like me so far?"

CHAPTER TWO

HOW I OVERCAME THE NAG

Walking down the street one day, I became aware of a constant chatter running through my mind. "Janice, you're not any good at (this or that). Why did you snap at your husband this morning? Who do you think you are?"

I got a sick feeling in my stomach. "Why can't I do anything right? What's going to go wrong today?"

It isn't very flattering. That nasty voice that hammers in your head and grabs your attention – it was all *NAG-i-tivity*. I felt as if I were pushing up against Mount Everest as this chatter demeaned and demoralized my every step.

I finally sat down on the curb and thought about what I was hearing from this vicious voice of doom and gloom. It was no wonder I couldn't accomplish my dreams. All I saw were the roadblocks that wore me down and sapped my energy.

As in the song, *Looking for Love in all the Wrong Places*, it dawned on me that I was looking for accomplishment in all the wrong ways. Because of my recent discovery of the 'NAG' and her relentless, ugly raving, I stopped and listened to her telling me how stupid I was ... and furthermore, how everything I said was ridiculous. She nit-picked and made me feel useless. Listening to her, how could I ever succeed?

Some of the comments I heard came in the sound of my mother's voice, or my brother's, or anyone else critical of me at one time or another – but most of all, they were the very things I'd said to myself over the years. Actually no one criticized me in any way that I hadn't criticized myself. Was this the way I felt about myself? Yes! I realized this was my own anger in a vocal form. I felt like a fiery volcano, erupting and spewing all of the disruptive, chaotic thoughts I possessed.

That's when I made a choice to stop. Stop listening to that NAG. Stop believing her. Stop living a life of limitation based on her false opinions that keep me from my heart's desire.

You Run, But You Can't Hide

My first impulsive reaction to solve my problem was to stay busy and keep giving, giving ... and giving some more. Surely *that* would drown her out. I had children, a home, a husband, a job, and a list of other demands that kept me on the move. If I stayed busy enough, I wouldn't have time to let this NAG-i-tive energy pull me into depression.

My 'to do' lists became longer and more hectic. I kept my life together in a web of frenetic energy accomplishing my next 'to do.' Later, I realized my *giving, giving, giving* was nothing more than a hollow imitation of *doing, doing, doing.* It wasn't coming from my heart and I wasn't *listening* to my **Divine Connection.**

Then there were times in the middle of the night that caught me unaware. NAG-i-tive thoughts filled my mind. They frightened me and made my heart sad. I couldn't stop them. These feelings made me feel scattered and unfocused during the day; brushing them under the rug made it more and more difficult to concentrate on my full 'to do' list. In the end, all I accomplished was facing more challenges and receiving fewer rewards. It didn't take long for me to feel worn out, useless, and unappreciated.

Things that should have been happy for me, tasks such as closing a big sale at work were nothing more than added aggravations. Instead of being happy about the commission check, I was burdened when the company doubled my sales objectives and gave me less territory. The only thing I focused on was, "I wasn't good enough."

Every time I achieved success, the NAG minimized my happiness with the thought that I would never be enough, and failure was just around the corner. Success always fell short of my expectations and needs. So, instead of building on my success, I allowed the NAG to rob me of any thought of accomplishment.

When I went home, the kids cried for my attention and time. I felt I needed to be at home for them and guilt-ridden because I couldn't be in two places at one time. My husband's needs and desires also called for my attention. I was pulled in many directions, feeling inadequate on all fronts. I wanted to be a great mom, good employee and a loving wife. I redoubled my efforts and made a commitment to be everything to everybody.

I learned to manage my time better. I took a course in time management, believing that if I became more productive, I would find the love and appreciation I craved. This allowed me to become super-mom.

I was up at 5 a.m. to take my daughter to ice-skating practice, rushed home, did the laundry, got to work on time and filled my appointment book with a double load of clients. I was never late in preparing dinner for my family. There were doctor's appointments, field trips, karate lessons, and soccer practice. After dinner, there was homework and housework, and a hard-working, loving husband who deserved my attention.

That's when it happened. It all fell apart one more time, and I had nothing left of myself.

Starting Over

I looked in the mirror and saw lines of stress, anger, frustration. The NAG was in control and that inner voice of NAG-i-tivity clamored. She was all I heard. "You'll never be any good at anything. You're a terrible mother, a bitchy wife. And you're a disaster at your job."

I took a deep breath. "Stop!" I yelled at the mirror. "You are a dreadful, ugly NAG. I can't take it anymore!"

Frankly, I thought I was losing my mind. It was the first time I talked back to myself with such conviction, but I'd suffered enough. The NAG-i-tive thoughts racing inside my head were a confirmation of this terrible, bitchy, awful person I felt was me. My NAG-i-tive thoughts had created a monster. I could actually see her – hair standing on end, the world on her shoulders, yelling and bitching with every step.

This was the NAG who made me feel afraid, defensive and sorry for everything I did or didn't do. The NAG who never took the blame, but was quick to dish it out. It was always my fault. She was a Neurotic, Anxiety-ridden Grinch. N – A – G!

She lived in my own thoughts. It made me shudder. Her only job was to tell me how terrible I was and to remind me I was dreadful. By the looks of me, she was doing a pretty good job. She tried to dominate my thoughts that morning and told me I didn't have love, romance, appreciation or whatever else I thought I needed in my life, because I wasn't good enough, smart enough, pretty enough, thin enough, rich enough, sexy enough, young enough, old enough, strong enough, nice enough, patient enough, talented enough, and so on. She added insult to my already injured self: "Your boobs are too small, your butt is too big and you need a facelift."

That was the last straw. I was going to find a better way to live. The demand for Goodness in my life *awakened* me. I needed to see myself from a different perspective. I wanted to be a better person. I thought I was loving, decent, and caring. What had happened? Wasn't that enough? In truth, I'd lost sight of that person; I believed what the NAG was saying about me. It had to stop.

I sat on the floor for what seemed to be hours, remembering what I wanted in my life, remembering who I was. Remembering how it felt to be loved and loving – happy and beautiful. I know it's radical, but I knew in my heart, this feeling was still true for me and everyone who's faced this kind of meltdown. My journey was the search to live the Goodness Experience and once again value myself.

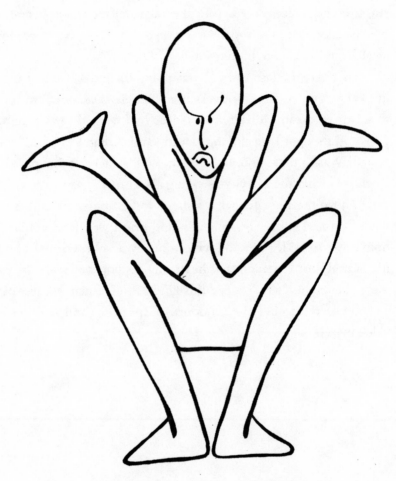

"Your hips are too wide. Your
muscle tone is flabby. And I'd
get a face-lift if I were you."

CHAPTER 3

THE DIVINE CONNECTION

Everyone has their own individual and unique *Divine Connection* and, as loud as the NAG screamed and tried to get her way, I knew I had to listen to that inner voice, the one who knew the person I yearned to be – poised, confident, humorous, strong. I had to re-discover this person I knew in my heart was me. I yearned for this higher source to guide me. Was it God? I didn't know, but it was Divine.

Everyone seems to have a God, regardless of religion. I have always felt there is a higher power, a source within each of us. I knew there was a voice of Goodness and love – a still, small voice I'd heard before, always trying to get my attention.

Then it dawned on me. This was my *Divine Connection* that had always given me the right answers even when I didn't want to listen. The voice that taught me to see my own value instead of allowing others to measure me with their opinions, needs, and wants. I also became aware that I needed to see the outside world not as the enemy, but as the expression of my own beliefs and thoughts. If I wanted a better life, I needed to monitor my NAG-i-tive thoughts.

I made the conscious decision after many stops and starts to see only Goodness in my life. Even when 'cold winds' blew through my life, this Good was all I wanted to hold to, to see and feel. I discovered my life was a tapestry of richness right at this moment, as unique and individual as my fingerprint or my DNA.

I didn't need to *wait* for someday, it was already NOW! Living in the NOW is the Goodness Experience. I didn't need to change anything; I just needed to awaken to the truth of what I was, who I was and where I was. I had to see myself as a unique expression of Goodness.

CHAPTER 4

WHAT ARE YOU THINKING?

As I began to talk with other women about how they dealt with life in the face of fear, obstacles, problems, and disappointments, I heard horror stories, tragedies of epic proportion that had scarred their lives.

I wondered how in the world a Goodness Experience could come to those who had been in circumstances far worse than I. Some women had suffered the loss of a spouse, or a child or a parent that had devastated their lives. Some women had been driven to the brink of their existence, had let their anger take control, and then had been imprisoned for breaking the law.

Each situation had its own desperation that made these women feel they had no other choice, so violence and misery had erupted in their lives. Some turned to drugs to numb feelings of anger and frustration. Many had faced betrayal, a loss of innocence that created a spiraling fall into depression, anxiety, a sense of abandonment, and a loss of self esteem.

I realized we've all had circumstances that claimed our innocence, some worse than others. It became clear to me, it did not matter what our past had been. At any time, each of us could make the choice to awaken to a Goodness that is inherently ours. We have the right to change what we think, change how we feel. We have the right to be free of the NAG! To awaken to this we *must* activate, allow, and accept Goodness, and become who we truly are!

I Think

If you see yourself as a small, insignificant person having nothing to offer the world, you'll get exactly what you believe and it won't be very happy or successful. This is where the Goodness Experience changed my perception. I quit listening to the NAG and made a conscious choice to allow only Good into my life. It was an honest *conviction* that gave me clarity and the power to see who I really was, and to know I had a *unique* and *individual* purpose. For the first time, I wasn't afraid to know my true self.

I realized I was not a mixed bag of unruly emotions, fueled by NAG-i-tivity. I started each day activating my Divine Connection and living freely from my heart. I knew this was the Goodness Experience.

Seeing 'me' in a new way, accepting and allowing only Good in my life, and listening to my Divine Connection began to change my experience. I didn't disregard the world outside; I listened to what others thought and I respected their thoughts, but I didn't let it rule my life. I chose to *listen* to my Divine Connection and *value* what I knew was true about myself. And I began to see others in a new light; we are all part of this Goodness Experience.

I was learning to rely on the Universal Laws of Good: my right to think and feel were my tools to express life in my own individual way. These laws are the principles of love, truth, honesty, and hope. They are laws we can depend on, Laws of Goodness that do not waver.

The Goodness Experience became my assurance I was divinely loved and this translated into *being* loved and *being* loving, cherished and protected. I accepted and expected that I had the *right* to allow only the best from the world around me ... if I *knew* only my best. I learned, when we live from these principles that are the very essence of love, what we give to ourselves and others can only be the best.

We normally don't take the time to honor this privilege in our lives. We neglect the most important and vital exercise – loving ourselves. If we don't exercise that love, without judgment and criticism, we can never see our world free of problems. First, I needed to accept I was doing the very best I could in every endeavor, every moment in every day. Next, I had to have the humility to grow and learn. This gave me the power to feel confident in this newfound knowledge.

It is a discipline of choice to always look to our heart for direction and listen for the steps to take in finding our fulfillment. Our Divine Connection is always found if we quiet the NAG, wipe away the MUD – Misery, Uncertainty, Doubt – and truly listen.

If we have made wrong decisions in the past, or suffered at the hands of others, we must *let it go*. And when I say *let it go*, I don't mean brush it off or sweep it under the rug. I mean forgive – love yourself and others. Don't NAG at yourself about the past or feel guilty. Don't allow resentment to linger. Just accept it was the best (he, she, or I) knew how to live at that moment. If it turned out badly, we learned from it. Whether we accept it or not, Good is always present when you *allow yourself to see it*.

NOW is the opportunity to realign from a fresh slate, the way we think, live and feel about our existence. If we hang on to

NAG-i-tive thoughts, we will have to live with them. We must get on with our lives and learn to forgive. Forgiveness is a great exercise that opens the heart to receive the love and freedom we deserve.

Here are a few stories from people who have learned from the Goodness Experience:

Staci's Story

Staci, a 62-year-old psychologist who has contributed her talents and knowledge to helping people for the last 30 years, was emotionally devastated when I met her. Her son was dying of AIDS and she felt abandoned and lost. All of her knowledge, talent and the love shared with others in her career meant nothing. She had helped others heal their hearts from broken dreams and broken lives, and now her own heart was broken.

As she spoke tearfully about her son, I softly reminded her of the beautiful power she held within her heart. In her son's time of need, she could become a beacon of light for him and for herself.

I shared with her the Goodness Experience of living from your heart. We talked about ways she could show her son how much she loved him, without dwelling on the tragic circumstance of his illness. She could make him laugh and remember the Goodness they'd always shared that could never be taken away from them. She was able to use her beauty, her power and her grace that were always with her, even in the face of tragedy. The expression of this pure gift of love would enrich both of them.

When she was reminded of her Goodness Experience that was always available to her, Staci's whole demeanor brightened. It did not minimize the sorrow concerning her son; it was an answer that gave her a purpose and opened a vista to share with him. Her sense of helplessness left her, and her voice, that previously trembled and shook, transformed into a quiet sound of strength and courage. She saw that she did hold a Grace and Goodness in her heart that healed others and would now heal her.

The Goodness Experience showed her how to survive the pain and make a positive choice by looking through a unique and different lens of reality.

Tanya's Story

Tanya was 38 years old and had never been able to establish a relationship with a man that lasted. Every man she attracted mistreated and abused her. She was a bright and beautiful woman with lofty ambitions; she was accomplished and successful in her job as an executive of a Fortune 500 company **but** she suffered from loneliness, feelings of inadequacy, and emotional pain from unfulfilling personal relationships that had created scars of fear and a lack of confidence.

She told me that in a room filled with hard-working, loving, and caring men, she could find the one loser in the group, the one who, on the surface, was exciting and intriguing ... needed her help. She would glow in his adoration. She would fix his problems and make his life a dream. Then her life would be perfect. Why did she always pick the loser? She attracted men who had their own inadequacies and she tolerated unloving relationships because it made her feel needed but never valued.

Tanya needed to learn to accept herself as the woman she was and not the woman of the NAG'S making. She would never be attracted to a man who was worthy until she stopped seeing 'inadequacies' in herself and others.

She needed to see her beauty, her Goodness, her intelligence as the woman she was now – not the one she yearned to be.

The Goodness Experience provided the way for her to activate her unique and fulfilling qualities. Tanya realized what the problems were. As she began to understand her true value, she was then able to accept and allow value in others.

When she timidly began to listen to her own expectations about life and value, and what she wanted in her world, she learned to make her decisions based on love, honesty, and truth – not on fear, anger, lack or ego. She consciously resisted the NAG, and began to live her Goodness Experience and enjoy the results of Goodness. Living and communicating the tenderness she had always felt within her heart, to herself and the world around her. She learned she didn't have to tolerate any abusive behavior from herself or others.

The men in her life started to treat her with the same respect she felt about herself. She was able to have healthy and committed relationships. Tanya made a conscious choice to trust her Goodness qualities of love and beauty and that choice reversed her situation. She found harmony in her values and actions bringing her peace and contentment.

Debra's Story

*Debra had it all. She was a woman who had gone through life in a charmed existence. She was popular, always had handsome boyfriends, married a successful man and had a beautiful daughter. Hers appeared to be an idyllic life **but** there came a day, a challenge, when her seeming 'good* luck' changed. She lost her husband, her home, and her money ... and it felt as if her entire life was destroyed. She became bitter, frightened and took on the posture of a victim, waiting for the next calamity. Do you blame her? She was in shell shock. Her anger manifested itself in the lines on her face and the indigestion in her stomach. She rarely smiled and continually complained about her unfortunate losses, lamenting, "Why me? What have I done to deserve this?"

Debra's only daughter suffered in the absence of her mother's former bright and confident self, as well as the loss of her father who had chosen to be with another family. Debra's daughter reached out for an illegal drug called Ecstasy. The frustration along with the effects of drugs escalated their mother-daughter relationship into violence. Volatile battles of one will against another filled every conversation. There were recriminations, regrets and blame that did nothing to solve their communication problems.

When I first spoke with Debra, she was bitter, heartbroken and hopeless. Her life was one disappointment that stretched into the next. She was inconsolable. She talked to me about how she "used to be" – positive, upbeat, confident. Now life was too hard and too scary, and her past was where she tried to live in order to escape her pain. Her days were filled with fears about the future.

In our first few meetings, she had very little interest in hearing about a Goodness Experience. She was focused on her anger and resentment about how she had done everything 'right.' She'd been a good wife, a good mother, had given to charities, and done all the things that were supposed to assure her of happiness. Isn't this the formula we've been raised to believe? "What happened?" she kept asking.

"You gave to everyone," I agreed. "Why did you make those choices?"

"Because I loved doing those things for my family."

"Do you think that love isn't with you right where you are?"

She looked at me as though I had stabbed her through the heart. Then her expression changed to rage. "I sure as hell don't feel there is love anywhere. Do you think I would choose these terrible things to happen to me?"

I sat silently and listened. She looked at me and pushed away from the table, petulantly crossing her arms. I had struck a chord that she didn't want to discuss. "Debra, it's a fact that bad things happen to good people. But, regardless of what circumstance you are in, you always have control, and your control always comes from love," I said. We each have a unique journey in life and a purpose to fulfill. That journey is not always easy, but right where you are, at this moment, it is filled with the same love, creativity and abundance you've always possessed."

She shook her head defiantly, but I continued, "What we accept in our thinking we manifest in our lives. Our beliefs make up the direction, the feeling and the power that propel us through our day. Your anger and resentment has been a NAG-i-tive drag on your life. "

"How could that be? I've tried so hard to make the best of this horrible situation."

All Debra could see was misery. The NAG was in control.

As we talked about her marriage and life of the past, Debra saw how she had been dissatisfied in her marriage and was trying to make the best of that also. She had felt unfulfilled even before her life fell apart, and this feeling had tainted everything in her relationships.

After a lengthy discussion, she admitted to me she had wanted out of her marriage. This was not something she could face so she blamed every difficult circumstance on someone or something out there, making herself a 'victim' and gaining the attention she craved.

Debra began to see how her unresolved desires had sabotaged her marriage, her life and her career. As she sat, arms still crossed and resistant to answers, she clearly saw herself as that victim.

I asked, "Who do you think you are as a person?"

She burst into tears and shook her head. She had no idea anymore.

"How did you feel about yourself five years ago?"

"On top of the world," she answered.

"Would you like to be there again?"

Her answer was, "Yes, of course!"

Step-by-step, Debra and I worked at developing an understanding of her Goodness qualities, and she began to see her Goodness Experience. She had to let go of her identity of being a victim in order to recognize she had power over her thoughts and feelings. She had to learn to listen to her Divine Connection and watch the unfolding of Good. When she talked about her life before, it was filled with love and truth and beauty. She had experienced her Goodness for years and, by listening to her Divine Connection today, she'd learned she could never again lose herself to the NAG.

She is once again successful, happy and on top of the world. This time, she knows where her value comes from and lives in the lush tapestry of her life that can only come from relying on the ever-present Laws of Goodness.

"er ... mm ... h e l p ... e e e k ..."

CHAPTER 5

GOOD IS IN
EVERY MOMENT OF OUR LIFE

Keep Your Focus

The Laws of Goodness are always active, supporting and sustaining you. They are the proof that God or Good is present in our lives.

Disappointments and hardships can be 'angels' that motivate us to discover Goodness in every circumstance. We have to learn we are never in a helpless position. At any time, we can awake to the Good we value about ourselves and others and live life more fully. We can look at our problems as opportunities to move forward with courage in the path of our heart's desires.

The choice is *always* ours. Only the NAG would try to stop us and keep us in the MUD of despair and failure. Ask yourself:

* Will you accept being a victim, or will you have the courage to make your own positive choice?

- · Will you allow yourself to overcome fear, loss, and grief and pursue a career of success?
- Will you let go of the anger, the bitterness, the hatred that life's tragedies have fostered?
- Will you allow yourself to look at your reality differently?
- Will you allow yourself to come out of the state of self-pity and quit asking, "Why me?"
- Will you release the beliefs of, "Nothing good ever happens to me?"
- Will you stop asking, "Who do I think I am to reach for success?"

Or ...

Will you choose the Goodness Experience?

It Takes a Conviction from the Heart

You can be sure the NAG will never disappoint you, and you can depend on her to make your life miserable. Or you can make a choice to live a life you've always desired. A life where you have the tools to overcome your misery, your MUD and your NAG: A life with your very own heartfelt thoughts guided by your Divine Connection that is always with you.

If this is what you want, the answers lie in the exercises that follow.

- Love more deeply.
- Laugh more fully.
- Live more freely.

Now who wouldn't want that?

Discover Your Goodness Experience!
21 Days to Fulfillment!

⇨ The Goodness Experience is about living in harmony, finding fulfillment in your career of life.

⇨ Discovering your individual uniqueness and finding purpose in daily existence.

⇨ Exercising your inherent ability to activate, allow and accept the life that you yearn to experience.

⇨ Tap into your Divine Connection that will influence your life and open the doors of a reality to live, love and enjoy.

⇨ Activate the real you, valuing who you are and expressing love in every moment of every day.

⇨ This is not a Utopian journey without obstacles; but it is your opportunity to answer the challenges of everyday living and fill every moment with success.

Overview of Days

Week One: ACTIVATE GOODNESS

Day 1: What if? (expand your horizon)

Day 2: I am gratitude (gives you power)

Day 3: I am Value (gives you purpose)

Day 4: I am Humility (the ultimate love)

Day 5: I am Beautiful (true wholeness)

Day 6: I am Love (true substance)

Day 7: I am Me (True being)

Week Two: ALLOW GOODNESS

Day 8: The Face of Fear

Day 9: The Tapestry

Day 10: Trust

Day 11: Acting On Your Desires

Day 12: A Goodness Date

Day 13: Grab Bag Day

Day 14: Living From Your Heart

Week Three: ACCEPT GOODNESS

Day 15: Cherishing Your Gifts

Day 16: Listening and Seeing

Day 17: Being Free

Day 18: Do's and Don't's

Day 19: Nixing the Nag

Day 20: Goodness, Poise and Humility

Day 21: A Miracle a Day Keeps You on Your Way

Twenty-one days = Trusting Your Divine Connection
ULTIMATE GOAL:
GAG THE NAG FOR GOOD!
and
LIVE IN HARMONY...

DAY 1: What If?

Goodness Purpose

- Breaking barriers.
- Expanding horizons.
- Seeing a new reality.

Goodness Action

- Make a list of the wildest, most outlandish "What if's?"
- Use your imagination and have fun.

When you start your day, ask yourself: "What if things were different? What if I could feel freedom from the burdens, travails and challenges? What if I could change my world? What if I could be a better person? What if I could feel better? What if I could have harmonious, positive relationships with my friends, my spouse, family and with my business associates? What if I could be free of anger, resentment and frustration?"

There are 1001 "What-if's?" we yearn for in our lives. And there are 1001 "Yes, I can" answers awaiting your discovery. Today, we're going to start bringing our "What-if's?" into reality.

We all dream, think and sometimes obsess about making our lives better. The real question is: How do we put these into reality? Do you ever wonder about the possibilities of what you want, what you need, and how you might fulfill your life and have the courage to see them become reality? What if all your problems were gone? Then what?

Today is your day to think about all the "What if's?" in your life and start seeing them in the context of "What I *desire* is _____."

"What if?" takes your desires out of dreaming and obsessing, and thinking about them. "What if?" lights the way and opens your heart to the Goodness Experience.

This simple exercise flexes your muscle of seeing what you desire as possible, expanding your horizons by focusing on what you want for yourself and the world around you. When you listen to your highest sense of Goodness, it will open the way for new beginnings and a better way of life.

We sometimes get so caught up in the everyday demands, the NAG accomplishes her purpose, and we lose track of our lives and find ourselves in the spiraling NAG-i-tivity of circumstance. Today, we can stop and listen to our heart's desire, feel the power of our Divine Connection, and see Goodness in our life by imagining "What if?"

Listening from Your Heart

What we yearn for in our life is our heart's desire. Most of us rarely take the time to listen to what we want. And if we do, we feel selfish and self-centered. At least, that's what the NAG would have us think.

Listening to our Divine Connection allows us a discovery of all the Good we need: *It is to realize who we truly are; and to love the world around us.*

The first time I thought about: "What if I could be the person I've always yearned to be?" or, "What if I could be happy?" another thought toppled on top of that one. The answer came clearly and calmly: "You do have all you *want*. You are the person you yearn to be; *you're just not seeing it.*" This was a positive answer I knew was my Divine Connection.

Then I shrugged sarcastically and said to myself, "Sure, how can I have and be all that I want and not even see it?" Well, I stopped and tried to listen again for my Divine Connection and I heard *the voice* that guided me into my Goodness Experience. How did I know that voice? It is the one that's always positive and uplifting and reassuring.

That's when other thoughts hit me:

- If I'm not experiencing what I want, maybe I'm not looking in the right direction.
- Do I really want to be better or do I just want to talk about it and blame others?
- Do I want to cling to my past inadequacies, cry about them or grow out of them?
- Do I really want to be more successful or do I just want to wallow in my failures?

After all, it is a lot safer and easier. Okay, I had to decide and commit to what I wanted. Now, I'm going to ask you a lot of questions, the same ones I had to ask myself.

The Questions

"What if you allow yourself to be totally and unconditionally confident in the midst of a crisis?"

Is your answer, "That would be ridiculous. How can I be unconditionally happy?" You can if you stop listening to the NAG and allow opportunity to appear in every moment of your life.

"What if you focus on the opportunity right where you are standing, regardless of the circumstance that seems so dire?"

Stay with me on this: What if you work to see what is right about NOW, and refuse to allow NAG-i-tivity to enter this moment. Rather than dwelling on what is wrong today and yesterday, and planning on what will be wrong tomorrow, focus on what is right. Seize your opportunity.

Remember, you govern your world with your own thinking. If you want Good, focus on Goodness. If you want bad experiences, then go ahead and focus on your NAG.

It's always your choice.

"What if you allow yourself to wake up in the morning and feel a surge of energy and certainty of Goodness for today?"

In the past, I woke up in the mornings, especially when I couldn't sleep because of worry the NAG had created, so filled with a sense of dread, I knew I had to change that nasty NAG habit, and I did.

"What if you decide to wake up and be generous with yourself, your family, your co-workers?"

"What if you decide to *activate, allow* and *accept* that today will be a great day?"

"What if you wake up with the conviction that today is *already* a great day, even if your NAG says you won't have a good day?"

I changed that NAG habit with the conviction from the heart to pause and challenge any bad thought that came my way. When I made a conscious choice to awaken to the Good that awaited me in every moment of every day, I knocked the NAG right off her pompous perch of smugness. I wouldn't accept the MUD.

When this thought to deny the NAG's demands came to me, at first I didn't believe it either. Trust me on this, it works.

Now let's take this one step further ...

"What if, in the middle of a tumultuous situation, you could maintain your poise and composure and not allow a circumstance to bring you down? What if you refuse to allow your emotions to run away with frustration and anxiety, even though you fear the worst." Can you imagine, in the middle of a fight between you and your spouse; or you and your boss; or you and your son or daughter; you could be the voice of integrity that leads to a solution? It's possible.

The following stories will show you how the "What-if?" exercise opened the Goodness Experience for these people.

Kelly's Story

Kelly had a partner in business who was very talented but overbearing. She was almost as close to him as she would have been to a brother, but there were times he could push her hot buttons to the point she never wanted to work with him again. Somehow they had survived several years of battling and tormenting one another. It was an unhappy and unhealthy relationship.

Kelly wanted to change it, but wishing it so wasn't going to work. When she tried to discuss the problem, he always left her feeling everything was her fault. This would make her feel as though she were the lowest form of humanity on earth. Barbs would be exchanged, and the uglier he got, the uglier she got.

"What if I could change the behavior within that relationship? What if I could find harmony within our business relationship?" When hell freezes over, she thought to herself. She had no control over him; he was independent, stubborn, monopolized conversations; thought he knew everything about everything. She knew he was smart and well respected in his line of work but she could no longer tolerate his behavior. She wasn't going to be his 'whipping boy' any longer.

One morning the phone rang; it was her partner and a fight erupted. After he finished yelling at her, she slammed down the phone. He was angry at her about something she had no control over and was not responsible for, and she had shot back a few comments in defense of the situation. She had tried to stay calm, but inside was an anger that felt as though she had been slammed up against the wall and cornered like a caged animal. It was the kind of anger that drains you and torments you, and all you can hear are the NAG'S recriminations. The fire was raging inside her brain.

Then she stopped in the middle of her NAG's anger and said, "What if I forgive?" She almost screamed it to herself until the fire of anger was out. 'Kaput'. It was gone!

Kelly realized you can't feel or say, "I forgive" without also experiencing love. She discovered it opened her heart to love. When she said "I forgive," it was not from arrogance or a 'holier than thou' moment. It was saying, "I forgive myself, I forgive him and I forgive the circumstance." It was a softening – a way to see beyond the rigidity of self-righteousness.

Kelly knew this was the Goodness Experience. She had listened to her Divine Connection, in spite of the raging anger. It Had Worked! In the midst of the tumultuous fight, she found harmony within their relationship through loving herself and him.

This was the first day of her Goodness Experience and she never wanted it to end. She also realized, when she asked, "What if?" she opened the door to feeling, saying and seeing forgiveness in her heart. She had transformed the anger between them into understanding. When she forgave, the burden of hate had vanished. She saw that beyond their harsh words were two people who wanted the same result: Goodness.

"What if I could do this whenever I'm angered, frustrated, or feel resentment about anything?" Kelly had expanded

her horizon and glimpsed the Goodness Experience. She
further decided anger had no place in her life. Prior to this,
she had tried to become numb, not realizing how angry she
was on a daily basis – not just about him, but about everything.

At that moment, she committed to a new way of responding to life – by not reacting. When she found herself in any
situation of anger, she began to practice forgiveness immediately, and it always led to compassion and understanding. She no longer allowed anger to fester into resentment
and then misery. She gained respect for herself and others
by understanding everyone in life feels they are doing the
best they can; this was something she learned to love
about human nature. She refused to allow, in her thinking,
a belief that her partner was an evil, unloving, and un-
grateful tyrant. She chose to see him as he truly was; a person of integrity. Once she stopped seeing him as the enemy, their relationship naturally became harmonious.

Kelly was on her way to trusting the Goodness Experience.

Carol Ann's Story

Carol Ann felt everything in her life was hard and this is
how the NAG held Carol Ann hostage: "I don't get any easy
breaks. I don't like to count on anything, and when I do, I'm
setting myself up for disappointment. It's always been like
that. But, what else can I expect?"

Carol Ann was in her fifties; a moderate success in her
chosen field in spite of NAG-i-tive thoughts about herself.
Her energy was always sapped, her expectations were always tempered by NAG-i-tivity, and she rehearsed a never-
ending litany of the difficulties she faced. These NAG-i-tive
thoughts prevented her from feeling Good about who she
was and how she was.

I often wondered, if she could hear her complaints played back to her, would she realize that the NAG had her on the mat and was about to win the match of life vs. death, Good vs. bad, happiness vs. depression, success vs. failure? Carol Ann took mood elevators that swung her from ecstatic to the depths of depression. Ay-yi-yi! Elevators that went up and down.

What about her Goodness Experience? After she read about "What If?" she wondered if she could wake up and realize that her thoughts govern her experiences. "What if?" she attached her thoughts to the Laws of Goodness and never again became a victim? She had spent too many years in her life waiting for the other shoe to drop—waiting for tragedy to come to her.

By integrating the Goodness Experience into her life, Carol Ann increased her Goodness certainty for life. She hasn't yet accomplished all her "What if?" questions, yet the Goodness Experience has opened up an entirely new way of thinking for her. And her list of complaints have all but vanished from her conversations and transformed into counting her successes.

We all take life one step at a time, and Carol Ann is progressing with her new way of thinking, seeing and feeling.

Karen's story

Karen never knew life without stress and worry about money. She grew up in a family of six children, and it seemed they always lacked the funds to feel comfortable. Everything was a struggle to make ends meet. She started working when she was eleven, cleaning houses and baby-sitting for the neighbors. As she grew up, she taught art and painting, and helped her father in his business on the weekends. All of these tasks deprived her of playing with her friends, and her brothers always treated her like a misfit. At sixteen, she earned an art scholarship, but her family needed her to work and help pay the rent, so she had to turn down the scholarship. It made her feel deprived, or so said her NAG. An opportunity to advance had escaped her, and she began to resent these losses. Karen felt the Good in life was going to be taken away from her, especially if she didn't have money. She felt imprisoned and burdened by her impoverished thoughts.

Karen finally managed to get through college and find a good job, but her financial picture didn't change. She had not released her 'poverty thinking,' was still in turmoil and felt deprived of the happiness she thought she deserved.

Once she graduated, she accepted a job in a very high pressure corporate structure with a volatile sales environment. Each day was a risk and constant fear if her sales quotas weren't met. This constant worry about job layoffs, corporate politics, and shifting economies eroded her ability to excel.

When she married, her problems magnified. Her husband was an entrepreneur whose line of work was always a gamble. Karen, through the years, became short-tempered and worn out. Her NAG had taken over when she began to read about The Goodness Experience.

Day One was Karen's wake-up call to ask herself, "What if I could live without the constant NAG of never having enough money, time, or energy?"

At first, it was almost impossible for Karen to imagine there was even a choice. The NAG was busy running her into the ground. "If you hadn't spent so much on your house – if you had bought a more economical car – if you hadn't spoiled your kids – you know you don't deserve any of those nice things – they're just putting you into debt."

After all of these NAG thoughts, Karen couldn't bring her-self to think about the question, "What if I had all the money I needed?" The NAG had drowned that thought long ago, and succeeded in making Karen feel guilty and unde-serving.

The Goodness Experience taught her to discipline her thought to activate, allow *and* accept *a "What if?" shutting out the NAG-i-tiv-ity. She realized it wasn't only money she needed. She realized what she most needed was to love herself and listen to her Divine Connection. This translated into having every need met. It wasn't the material objects she needed to possess to make her feel better – it was al-lowing and accepting a renewed sense of who she was and what she was that would meet her needs. Karen expanded her horizon and found her true source of Goodness. Wasn't that what she really was looking for? Goodness from her heart answered doubt, insecurity, and anxiety.*

Activating Your Goodness

Make your own list of "What-if's?" and define how they will make your life better. Go ahead. Let go of the barriers and imagine anything you want. It's your list and your world. Always remember, the Goodness Experience takes place one step at a time. Be patient and enjoy the process.

_____
_____
_____
_____
_____
_____
_____
_____
_____
_____
_____
_____
_____
_____
_____
_____
_____
_____
_____

Gag the NAG For Good

GOODNESS NOTES

**You are Great ... You are Marvelous ...
You are Magnificent!**

_____

_____

_____

_____

_____

_____

_____

_____

_____

_____

_____

_____

_____

_____

_____

_____

_____

_____

_____

_____

_____

_____

_____

GOODNESS NOTES

You are Lovely ...

_____

_____

_____

_____

_____

_____

_____

_____

_____

_____

_____

_____

_____

_____

_____

_____

_____

_____

_____

_____

_____

_____

_____

GOODNESS NOTES

You are Beautiful ...

_____

_____

_____

_____

_____

_____

_____

_____

_____

_____

_____

_____

_____

_____

_____

_____

_____

_____

_____

_____

_____

_____

_____

_____

_____

THE NAG RULES!

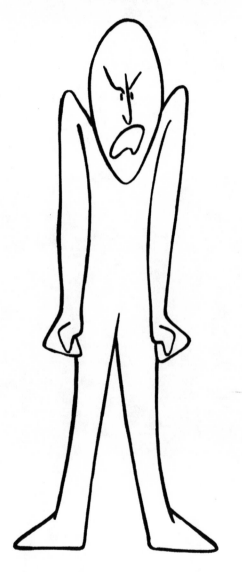

**"Go ahead, make my day – FAIL!
This is a waste of time."**

DAY 2:   I Am Gratitude

Goodness Purpose

- Living your abundance.
- Feeling love – Being love – Experiencing love.
- Acknowledging your Divine Connection.

Goodness Action

- Stand in front of a mirror and acknowledge your Goodness – physically and spiritually.
- Your Divine Connection will lead the way.
- Love yourself, acknowledge your power.
- Know that gratitude brings you FREEDOM! (Do it even if you don't believe it. You'll see why later.)

Have a Goodness day!

I recognized that being fully alive required the *action* of gratitude – "I am gratitude." The person I yearned to be was loving and grateful with every beat of my heart to everyone, in every moment, with an overflowing and abundant sense of being I knew as freedom. I wanted to see this Law of Gratitude functioning and operating throughout my day. That was the life I wanted – a life experienced in a complete circle of fulfillment.

I had learned a lesson at this point about the wholeness of my Goodness Experience and the powerful and positive influence of gratitude. When I was living Gratitude, I accepted and knew that every problem could be solved. It was as though I was looking through a new lens – my life was in harmony when I was grateful, when I saw the truth and the power of this activity. I could not be angry, sad or discouraged. Gratitude fueled my existence and I knew I could accomplish anything. As I brought a clearer understanding of appreciation and purpose to my life, my business flourished.

BUT, WHEN I LISTENED TO THE NAG ...

My morning began with doubt, fear and worry. I was into anxiety, already rehearsing my day of obstacles. From the moment I opened my eyes, there was little time to think of myself as grateful.

On those mornings, I thought, *This is really crazy. How can I be grateful when I have nothing to be grateful for? Uh-oh, here I go again. I already know it. I'm listening to the NAG.* What was stopping me from naturally reaching out to my Goodness Experience that was always available and as near as a thought?

I had to solve this problem. I needed to be totally honest with myself. And, you guessed it, again, it was the NAG keeping me focused on NAG-i-tive, nasty, and hurtful thoughts that prevented me from seeing my gratitude found in Goodness.

The NAG convinced me I had nothing to be grateful for. After all, I had failed at things I wanted to do. I was working at a job I didn't like and felt guilty about not spending enough time with my kids and family. I knew my husband's family believed I was a failure as a wife and a mother. So, the NAG, and *everyone else* must be right. Most of all, I was a failure in my own eyes. I loathed my inadequacies and I didn't believe that I even had the *right* to feel grateful. How could I? It would be idiotic to be grateful for who I was because, in my opinion, I was nothing.

I thought for a moment and realized every circumstance I was in seemed to make it impossible for me to be grateful. And then I caught myself in this NAG-i-tive downward spiral of thought. I didn't like what my NAG-i-tive thoughts were saying. I heard myself blaming problems on myself and others: "Well, if I didn't have to work and support my family, since my husband isn't making enough money ..." or, "If people were nicer at work, maybe I would have something to be grateful for," or, "If my husband's family only knew what I have to deal with every day – bill collectors calling, the grade school assigning me one more task." Well, maybe then they would understand and I might have something to be grateful for. Why isn't everyone around me just a little more understanding? That would help.

I may have been justified in feeling these things. I may even have been right, according to the false picture I was buying. And the NAG did a very good job of keeping me churning during the midnight hours about all of these things. The NAG was at her best when I was tired and unprepared for her assaults.

One morning after a long night of turmoil, I questioned this line of self-blame and criticism. *Will it accomplish anything other than making me miserable? What am I thinking? Does everything have to be perfect in order to feel grateful?* I would have to wait forever. I knew this wasn't right.

The NAG would like to keep us in 'drama queen' mode whenever possible. And it was even comforting for a while when I felt I was the heroine being victimized – a real romance novel. What have I done to deserve this? (Did I mention guilt is another tool of 'NAG-i-tivity?') I realized I got an adrenalin rush when I felt like a martyr, a damsel in distress. I had used this manipulative effort far too long; it had begun to make me feel useless and vulnerable.

I wanted to throw water in my face. I was addicted to the NAG. I was buying *her* picture of who I was.

Getting Off the Rush

"I am gratitude" kept coming to me once I realized what a trap I'd fallen into. I thought about this for a moment. Gratitude is appreciating. Gratitude is seeing Good everywhere. Gratitude is a conscious acknowledgement of the Law of Goodness.

A reliance on this truth gave me the discipline to see Good as always present. I had to learn to see Good beyond any limited picture of lack or misery holding me hostage. Goodness was a silent and grateful acceptance of myself as a full and complete person because I understood my higher purpose: *I am gratitude*.

Okay, I said to myself in a trembling voice as I made a mental list, *I appreciate today is Friday*. I could feel myself smiling and saw that simple act of smiling as power – the power of love that I could rely on. (I know this may seem elementary, but smile and you will feel the Law of Goodness.)

I went to the drawer in the kitchen and pulled out a piece of paper and grabbed a pencil. Before I knew it, through the Law of Goodness, I found the lens of gratitude allowing me to appreciate and cherish everything in my life. Things I took for granted became visions to treasure. (It's funny how the MUD obscured my vision.)

I started another list, headed, "What I appreciate about myself." There was stone silence. *Surely there's something I appreciate about myself*, I thought. I almost felt embarrassed and I certainly was intimidated. The NAG continued her degrading comments.

I shut her down when I listened and wrote, "I love the way I look today." I didn't believe it but I said it anyway. Once I claimed I was grateful for my very being, I saw a dimple in my smile that I liked.

To think I had allowed the NAG to make me believe I was something ugly. I wanted to go further, not only appreciating the outside of my body but what I appreciated on the inside. I started listening. The NAG continued to try to regain my attention, but I refused. I yelled, "Aha! My true beauty is within!"

Another moment of gratitude came to me: *I like my courage.* I recognized that I was expressing courage in trying to overcome the NAG-i-tive thoughts that had hampered my life for far too long. When I looked at myself now, I suddenly saw uniqueness in my perception of the world and myself, I felt gratitude.

For the entire day, whenever I was met with a NAG-i-tive thought, I yelled out something I was grateful about. Just the fact I could be grateful and rely on this wonderful Law of Goodness opened up an entirely new way of thinking and experiencing.

I immediately felt light-hearted and happy. I felt freedom beyond anything I'd ever imagined and discovered I didn't have to wait for an event, a date, or a possession to feel gratitude. *"I Am Gratitude"* flowed through every moment when the Law of Goodness was my foundation. I was buoyant. I laughed more freely that day and I loved more deeply, as I felt the overflowing fullness of gratitude.

This new understanding of gratitude allowed me to enjoy every moment. I was living the Goodness Experience. There were some ups and downs, but I began to learn the discipline that brings freedom – "I Am Gratitude."

A Reminder...

I Am Gratitude is seeing only Goodness. This takes discipline and practice. It takes saying it when you don't believe it. You are turning your perception around; you are turning gratitude into a flowing river of love and life. There is something contagious about Gratitude. It stays with you even when you're unsure. It really is your best friend.

How Susie Activated Gratitude

"Yeah, sure," Susie said. She looked at me with insolence in her eyes, her body language defensive and her tone of voice combative. "The Goodness Experience is just a lot of happy thoughts. But, what do thoughts have to do with all of my problems?"

My heart ached for her. She had told me the story of her life earlier at the Goodness Experience workshop.

She continued, "I was raised to believe I could have anything I wanted and accomplish anything I desired. My parents were wonderful and always supported me in everything. But, my parents were older and had passed away by the time I was nineteen. They left me with money, but I didn't know how to handle finances and I spent it all on things I thought would make me happy. I was trying to fill the hole I felt in my life and tried to buy people to be my friends, stay with me, and go places with me. I started to drink a lot because I felt anxious and timid in crowds. The rest is the same old story and I ended up with nothing. My friends vanished when I didn't have money and now I'm alone. I feel ugly, unwanted and useless."

"Who told you that you were ugly?" I asked.

"Nobody has to tell me," she snorted, with a heavy dose of sarcasm. "I feel ugly." She looked at me with NAG-i-tivity.

"But, you're not," I said. "Your gratitude is your beauty."

"I don't understand."

"Tell me how you feel when you look at your two kittens?" I asked.

Her face softened. "I love them. I think they're the cutest."

"And, do they think you're ugly?"

She laughed and her face lit up. "Of course not! They love me!"

'That's your first step. Be grateful for their love. This is where your never-ending source of Goodness begins. That is the Goodness Experience, and you can always be grateful if you're willing to allow it, trust it and rely on it."

Susie used that simple moment to begin her journey and today, she has released her anger and resentment. She is living her Goodness Experience.

Phyllis' Story

Phyllis came to the Goodness Experience workshop because she was desperate for a change. She was overweight, worn out and a picture of the NAG's frustration. Phyllis had difficult challenges that wouldn't be easy for any of us; she was a caretaker for both her invalid mother and her handicapped son. She worried about them from the time she rose in the morning until she laid her weary head on her pillow at night.

The "what if?" day had been enlightening, enabling her to allow her desires to surface, but Phyllis hit a roadblock when she thought about gratitude. It was apparent that the NAG had her total attention as she stared at the blank sheet, wondering what in the world she had to be grateful about.

Her days began with uncertainty. "What if something bad happens to my son today?" This was always her first thought which led to another, and another NAG-i-tive result.

"What if I lose my job and can't pay my rent?"

"What if I can't be there for my mom?"

All she could think about was what might go wrong. This is the NAG's favorite addiction – fears that keep you in an anxiety-ridden state of mind. She had no time to think about appreciating the Goodness already in her life. She had no time to even think about herself. All of her energy and devotion was spent on just getting through her day.

If we put ourselves in Phyllis' shoes, we can certainly understand her dilemma, but her problems were almost life-threatening and she needed some real answers.

Phyllis needed an understanding of her Divine Connection – to know she was never alone, regardless of her fears and trials. She had to allow and accept there was always an answer, and that answer came from her understanding of a Supreme Goodness or God that is always present. I knew she could find answers by listening to her Divine Connection.

Phyllis was in tears as we sat across from one another. She wanted so badly to experience her Goodness that I had talked about earlier in the day during the Seminar.

"Phyllis, what if you could see only Good in yourself and others?"

"Wouldn't that be wonderful," she said, tearfully. "Is that possible?"

"Yes, it is. Because that's all there really is."

She looked confused. "But, what about all the things I've just told you about?"

"If you accept that picture of your life, you'll experience the very things you fear."

"How do I stop?"

"Let's start by doing something radical. What are you grateful for?"

After a long silence, she said, "My son. That he's alive, after his accident."

"That's Good. What else?"

"My job." This time she said her words with conviction.

"Why?" I asked.

"Because I know what I'm doing and I feel accomplished at the end of the day."

I saw her relaxing with this exercise of gratitude.

We sat and talked for a while about the activity of being grateful and understanding the power in this spiritual law of love. Before she left, she had one more thought about gratitude: "What if I always focused on gratitude ..." she asked, as her eyes lit up, "... and realized everything that seems imperfect is really a 'lie' manufactured by fear?"

Gratitude was already accomplishing its purpose. Phyllis had made a giant leap of understanding. She looked at me and gave a huge sigh of relief. Her shoulders relaxed and she smiled. "You know what this means? It means I don't have to live in fear any longer."

Gratitude was a step that came naturally and easily. Phyllis knew the Law of Gratitude was constantly alive in her thinking. She didn't have to voice it; she could experience it everyday. She had spiritually erased the fears of hopelessness she had held on to for many years and replaced them with a sense of ever-flowing Goodness that is gratitude itself.

Results are always the proof of the validity of any theory. Phyllis' results were extraordinary. She lost over 150 pounds and was selected for an extreme make-over program. Phyllis had known all along that fixing the outside was useless unless she fixed the emptiness inside. Gratitude filled her emptiness and opened the door to love. Love *was what she yearned for, and love was what she saw in everyone and everywhere.*

Connie's Story

This is what Connie shared with me about her gratitude experience:

"I was at work one morning and the thought came to me, 'I'm in a terrible mood.' I shrugged it off. As the day wore on, I became more irritable with every event. By mid-morning, I felt like a caged animal ready to attack.

"I felt discouraged. I knew this wasn't the Goodness Experience I yearned for or that you'd spoken about. I thought, How can I get out of it?

"Immediately, I looked around to see something Good happening right now! I had on my favorite sweater. Okay, that's Good, I thought. Then I heard a chime at one of the other employee's desk. I liked that sound. I didn't stop for the next ten minutes, looking around for more things to ignite the gratitude in my heart.

"I was experiencing Good around me and within me, the mental picture I had started with that morning was changing and my terrible mood dissipated. The Law of Gratitude was working and had changed my focus and that changed my experience. Gratitude was my 'quick-fix.'"

**"If I can't say anything BAD, I
just won't say anything at all."**

Activating Gratitude

Write below things that you are grateful for yourself and others:

Gratitude

GRATITUDE
FOR YOURSELF

I am grateful for:

_____

_____

_____

_____

_____

_____

GRATITUDE
FOR OTHERS:

I am grateful for:

_____

_____

_____

_____

_____

_____

GOODNESS NOTES

Gratitude is sexy!

_____

_____

_____

_____

_____

_____

_____

_____

_____

_____

_____

_____

_____

_____

_____

_____

_____

_____

_____

_____

_____

_____

_____

_____

GOODNESS NOTES

Think THANKS!

_____

_____

_____

_____

_____

_____

_____

_____

_____

_____

_____

_____

_____

_____

_____

_____

_____

_____

_____

_____

_____

_____

_____

_____

_____

_____

GOODNESS NOTES

What you appreciate...appreciates!

_____

_____

_____

_____

_____

_____

_____

_____

_____

_____

_____

_____

_____

_____

_____

_____

_____

_____

_____

_____

_____

DAY 3:   I Am Value

Goodness Purpose

- Value = Loving yourself!
- Value raises your expectations.
- Value is your treasure.

Goodness Action

- Let yourself go.
- Think about the people you admire.
- You are as valuable to this world as Aristotle, Leonardo da Vinci, the boss at work, the man or woman of your dreams.
- You are *value*. The Divine Connection guides you to your unique and valued identity.
- You are the treasure, so **live it**.

Discovering Your Value

I was having coffee with a friend one morning. "I don't know why I can't make more money," I told her. "I do a good job, but nobody ever gives me credit for my work and I never get a raise. I wish I could find another job."

My friend looked at me. "Why don't you give yourself a raise?"

"Yeah, right," I said, sarcastically.

"I'm serious," she said.

"What are you talking about?" I asked.

"Well, think about it. A raise is a symbol, not just for the money, but for recognizing your value. If you're not getting what you want, you need to see yourself as valuable. You've put the cart before the horse. You have to see more value in yourself and the rest will follow."

She was right. I didn't value myself, so how could I possibly see my work as valuable? I was so busy just trying to get through the day, I never took the time to value and appreciate who I was or to see the value of what I did in my job. In fact, I didn't think anything about me or my work was very special. I felt I was going through the 'motions' of living and working. Then I saw the problem clearly: "If I didn't value what I was doing, why would anyone else?"

This was the obstacle. I couldn't even think about valuing myself. If I did, the NAG would follow it with her reasons about why I wasn't valuable. And I bought into her NAG-i-tive ideas.

I persisted, knowing I must overcome the NAG's tirades. I turned to my Divine Connection which always assured me of my purpose and value.

But ...

My value seemed connected to everyone else's needs. My value was always measured by others. That was the NAG'S tool. If people liked me or didn't like me; if I got recognition for what I did at work or if I didn't ... I measured my value by other's opinions. I didn't see myself as a very interesting person. I didn't even like the person I saw in the mirror. This had to change.

These steps took courage. In fact, it took over a year before I was able to even consider my value, without looking to others to validate me. I had to see the little things I did in my job from a new perspective. I learned to appreciate the 'little things' that until now I'd accepted without seeing their value, without honoring every Good activity.

Once I started this new way of seeing things, I began to value everything, from going to the grocery store to making a great sale at my job. I could help others without feeling drained or swallowed up by them. I allowed my Divine Connection to guide me through every moment.

Then, I took it one step further. I saw these opportunities to see my value as gifts. I reasoned that we always value a gift, so I began seeing who I was, what I did and how I felt with a new sense of value, as gifts to cherish and share.

Who doesn't like continuous gifts? And because of my constant flow of value, I gave to others freely and abundantly.

At the end of the day, rather than being tired, I was newly energized. My new attitude and focus of valuing myself was a simple exercise shaping the uniqueness of who I was and how I experienced life. I had discovered my Goodness Experience.

THE NAG WAS IN A SNIT!

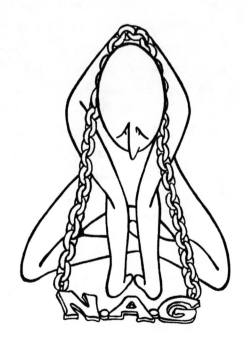

When I started to see things from a new viewpoint, the NAG became an enraged combatant. She would do her best to tear down my newly-found attitude. There were days I would become a NAG and lost my appreciation for myself. Yes, on those days, the face staring back at me in the mirror was lackluster, dull, upset, worried, tired and unhappy, dreading what the day held, and worrying about the future. My NAG caused my eyes to stop sparkling with excitement and pounded past failures of yesterday into my brain like a mantra. It clouded every minute of every day with MUD –Misery, Uncertainty and Doubt. MUD slanted my view of everything.

If that's where you are right now, take a deep breath and, for a moment, quiet the NAG and remember the reality of your true value – who you are and what you love. Focus on the gifts that *you* possess.

When you open the door for the NAG, this figment of belief tells you, "You're too dumb, too fat, too poor, too lazy, too busy, too much, too little, you'll never get it right." The NAG makes you eat too much and then tells you you're too lazy to work out. You get the picture? Stop her in her tracks and remember your *value*.

The NAG is an unwelcome guest in the house of consciousness, who can make you angry. She can make you lash out at those around you – anyone who gets in her way – including you. She blames you and everyone else for life not working out the way you wanted. To make matters worse, your NAG makes you feel guilt-ridden because of all of those NAG-i-tive and angry feelings. Where's the value in that?

When I think about the NAG, I can just see her angry self, screeching, preaching, with the world on her shoulders, yelling at you and everyone else. She never blames herself, only others whenever anything goes wrong. She is a:

NEUROTIC ANXIETY-RIDDEN GRINCH aka N.A.G.

Her only job in life is to tell you how terrible and valueless you are. She steals your dreams and hopes, and has a reservoir of NAG-itive ammunition. "Remember when ... you made the wrong decision ... chose the wrong date to the Prom ... acted like a brat ... got a divorce ... had an affair ... your boss got mad when you sent the wrong faxes."

She can pull out of the hat anything she wants and make it look as if you're the worst person who ever walked the earth. She takes anything Good that's ever happened to you and immediately makes you wonder if you really deserve it ... and if you do, what bad thing is going to happen next?

After a long and seemingly never-ending battle with the NAG, I finally asked myself, "Where is my *value* in this world?" Her NAG-i-tive chastisements had left me feeling empty, disconnected, unfulfilled and hopeless. She had made me feel foolish and ashamed, confused, stressed and overwhelmed. The NAG had won! I believed her.

So, if you look in the mirror today and don't see a joyful, happy face filled with love, hope and gratitude, take a stand for your *value!* Don't give in to the NAG. Make your choice – rely on your Goodness which is always with you and always valuable.

Everyone battles with the MUD (Misery, Uncertainty, Doubt) that the NAG throws at you. But, her rhetoric will become recognizable as a lie once you see your value. I knew that I couldn't listen any longer to her downgrading, always trying to stop me from feeling Good and valuing myself. Each time she tried to convince me I had no time to value myself – there were too many things to do, etc., etc., etc., – I consciously stopped and did the opposite of her demands. This was when I began to win and feel value in every moment.

Making Your List

What do you value the most? Your family? Your children? Your career? Your boyfriend? Your spouse? Your friends? Did you put yourself at the top of that list? If you didn't, you need to do that now. The most important and valuable asset in your life is *you!*

Discovering your value is accepting only the Good you see in yourself. It takes discipline to focus on Good. So today, pick out some things you value about yourself and the people around you. If the co-worker you don't like causes a problem, don't react to it; instead cherish a good quality about that person.

Always *respond* to your Divine Connection and never react to the NAG. Remember, focus on what you value about a situation, a person or yourself, and don't give any power to NAG-i-tivity. Make your list now.

_____

_____

_____

_____

_____

_____

_____

_____

_____

_____

_____

_____

_____

Enjoy Your Day with Value!

Mary's Story

Mary was totally confused. "My husband tells me I'm fat. He also says I'm lazy. To be quite honest, I'm tired of doing things for him because he never appreciates me. I'm tired of trying to please my boss who never appreciates me either. How in the world can I feel value about myself?"

"Everyone is valuable," I said. "Because who you are and what you are are totally unique and original. The source of your being is found in the qualities of Goodness. Your husband's value and your boss's value are just as important as your value."

"Well," she said petulantly, "I just don't see it. I think both of them are chauvinists. I wouldn't be fat if my husband would appreciate me. And I wouldn't be late for work if my boss appreciated me."

I couldn't go down that road with Mary. She was blaming everyone else for the choices she was making. She may be justified in feeling this way, but none of it was providing solutions for her. "Think about something you value in your life," I said.

Without hesitation, she said, "The marriage I once had."

"Well, have you ever thought about why that marriage was created in the first place?"

"We loved one another and I wanted to do everything for him. What was wrong with that?" Her tone had turned defensive.

"When did you stop valuing yourself as a wife?"

She looked shocked. "What do you mean?"

"I know from experience that problems start with our own belief about ourselves. You stopped valuing yourself as a wife and an employee long before your husband and boss stopped appreciating you."

After that, Mary started everyday consciously valuing herself before she got out of bed. She found her attitude softened and she began to shed the emotional eating habits that had added on extra pounds. As she learned to value her husband, he began treating her with the same respect she had for herself.

At work, Mary found herself being more helpful, contributing more to the projects she was working on, and her boss began to praise her work. Within a year of using the tools she learned from the Goodness Experience, she'd had several promotions, and her marriage returned to the loving relationship she remembered.

Sarah's Story

Sarah was a bright, beautiful, energetic, 23-year-old woman, working in a well-known retail establishment. She had been promoted to the position of Assistant Manager and was thrilled with the possibilities of climbing the corporate ladder of success. However, after facing many obstacles, she had lost her enthusiasm and faith in her abilities. She played the blame game when her shipments were late, and complained that her bosses were maniacs with their continuing demands on her to sell more, be more and do more. She was defeated when she came to the Goodness Experience workshop provided by her employer.

*Through the workshop, Sarah discovered her value by not allowing difficult circumstances to control her achievement possibilities. She saw, in her struggle to become successful, she'd forgotten the first step – **valuing herself**. She realized, when she didn't value herself, she fell into the trap of competing with her bosses, her co-workers, and practically every other person with whom she had a relationship.*

Sarah improved daily in her job by listening to her Divine Connection. Listening showed her how to communicate her ideas and find solutions to problems. She was able to see her value and to nurture value in others. Her work environment changed from chaos to harmony overnight.

Sarah learned that she did not have to accept any limitation. Once she awakened to her powerful value, she climbed that corporate ladder and is currently a regional manager in the corporation.

Robert's Story

Robert had just declared bankruptcy when I met him. Nothing could have been more demoralizing to him. He felt worthless and no longer able to function in the workplace. It was clear that he was embarrassed and felt he had no value as a person. He was a statistic in a world of loss, recriminations and failure.

I talked to Robert about starting from the very beginning. I suggested he had to throw out all the garbage the NAG had presented to him. He had to recognize his true self, the one he had always been, regardless of the problems that entangled him.

Robert had many reasons why he had fallen into his financial ruin, and we talked about the lessons he had learned. I pointed out to him those lessons had actually added value to him. By going through difficult experiences, we always progress forward.

"How am I progressing 'forward' when I've lost my house, my car, my job?"

"Moving forward and progressing are a Law of Goodness," I said. "Things that look so dire and disastrous can

*become 'angels.' Keep listening for your Divine Connection
and you'll see your progress. All of this is pushing you to
see value in yourself. Value is not from outside posses-
sions. Value is knowing yourself through your Divine Connection and listening. We come into this life with a promise
of happiness and fulfillment. Now, your responsibility is to
trust in that promise, lean on it, and it will lead you to your
value."*

*Several months later, Robert called to told me he had
made a wonderful transition in his life. He had found an
entirely new career that inspired him, and it was a career
he had always dreamed of, but felt he was not qualified
for. He was now living his Goodness Experience.*

Activating Value:

What do you value about yourself? (E.g., integrity, respect, honesty, etc.)

_____

_____

_____

_____

_____

How do you express this value?

_____

_____

_____

_____

_____

_____

GOODNESS NOTES

You're worth your weight in GOLD!

_____

_____

_____

_____

_____

_____

_____

_____

_____

_____

_____

_____

_____

_____

_____

_____

_____

_____

_____

_____

_____

_____

_____

_____

GOODNESS NOTES

You are priceless!

_____

_____

_____

_____

_____

_____

_____

_____

_____

_____

_____

_____

_____

_____

_____

_____

_____

_____

_____

_____

_____

GOODNESS NOTES

10 is perfection...You are infinite!

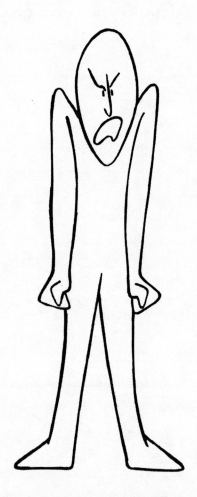

**"SHUT UP! I want what I want
NOW! And it's my way or no way."**

DAY 4:   I Am Humility

Goodness Purpose

- Focus on your Divine Connection ... Shhh ... Listen.
- Listen to your heart.
- Accept as fact, the answer you need is always complete and ever-present. When you think "I don't know," stop and listen. *Yes, you do know! Allow!*

Goodness Action

- Remember the deepest feeling of love you've ever felt in your life, a time when your world seemed to be in perfect harmony, living love without fear.
- Think about one of your underlying fears and dismiss it completely from your mind.
- Humility is experiencing life without fear.

When the word *humility* popped up in my mind, I wondered, *What does this have to do with the Goodness Experience?* Isn't humility something that makes you vulnerable. Gives people permission to walk all over you. Like being a doormat.

That was just what I didn't want, but this thought kept coming to me, so I took another look at *humility.* I discovered true humility was pausing, listening and focusing with a fresh approach. A *kneeling* to your Divine Connection. A yielding to see things the way your Divine Connection perceives the world. Opening up and allowing a new way of experiencing – with freedom.

In the past, I had often attempted to solve my problems by ruminating over them. I kept trying to find the solution over and over again in the same way, but I was going nowhere. Now I had learned humility was the way to overcome any obstacle on my journey to experience Goodness. I had to put it into Goodness action. I realized I had to see things from a higher sense of being, by *hearing and activating* my Divine Connection.

I knew I was caught up in re-acting to my NAG and all of the things others expected of me. All through my life, I'd heard nothing but the same old stuff echoing through my mind. But, how could I ever grow if I didn't get outside of the box that for me had made life a prison?

Humility was the answer. I had to listen for and activate my heart's desires. I discovered when I listened this way, I felt sure about my decisions. I was not *just* hearing my own human will. Once I allowed and let go of my inhibitions and my NAG-i-tive demands, I could see clearly what I needed to do. I also found that the decisions which came from relying on the Laws of Goodness were naturally accepted by the world around me. It was harmony I yearned for.

I practiced humility and learned to listen to my heart. It was a *light* that penetrated the darkness. I recognized almost immediately the NAG had a different way of dealing with happiness. She wanted it to come from an 'addiction' to a drama she created in my life. She wanted chaos to be the answer. With the *light* of humility, there could be only a positive manifestation of creation rather than chaos.

The NAG was fighting for her life – she loved chaos – but I realized that chaos came from darkness and led to destruction. She tried to convince me in my heart I really loved chaos. It was an adrenalin rush, but I knew this was only the flimsy substance of 'thrill-seeking.'

The NAG was very subtle in her ways. I wasn't even sure if I knew the difference between an adrenalin rush and happiness. Whenever I was unsure about this dilemma, I went for a walk. I wanted to find a contentment and understanding that I could trust. I realized I was so accustomed to chaos, I thought it was a natural way of life. I wanted to make the world around me a better place, but could I let go of my 'junkie chaos addiction' to the NAG and her subtle ways?

In many instances, when I came into a situation, I searched for and found problems. Was that a coincidence? Did it have to happen every time? Even when something Good happened, was I secretly expecting the other shoe to drop and experience something bad? Sadly, I realized I wasn't focusing on humility and hearing the Divine. I was watching the chaos and I wasn't building from a positive foundation. I allowed the NAG to stay in control. I had to turn this around. But how?

Seeing Good, All the Time, Everywhere, in Everyone

"I am humility." I realized by saying this, I was opening my thought to the Goodness in the midst of crisis. I kept repeating this phrase to myself when I came up against problems of any kind, *even if I didn't believe it.* It would have been so easy to lapse into chaos at times because it seemed so familiar and comfortable to me. When I was confronted with a difficulty that provoked, anger, frustration, hatred or any other NAG-i-tive feeling, I had to take a deep breath and say, "I forgive myself (or the other person) and this circumstance."

I thought about the Good I saw around me, and there were moments when it seemed impossible to find even a glimmer of Goodness. When things were difficult, I'd turn my palms toward the sky and quietly say, "S-s-s-s-s-s-h-h-h-h-h-h-h!" The NAG was clamoring and trying to grab my attention and cover me with MUD, but I disciplined my focus and listened for my Divine Connection. This was my road to freedom.

I was tired of the NAG and her weary ways and was ready to transform my thinking – to see a new way, a fulfilling and rewarding way by listening with humility. The NAG was finally quiet and I allowed only positive solutions, ideas, and reminders to come into my thought.

Down to the Detail

When you have a 'conflict' today, take a moment and go through the exercise of saying, "I am humility." Pause, listen and focus on your Good. Commit yourself to this idea and you will have the opportunity to find yourself and your happiness. It took me a little time to accept this proposition. I would find myself getting caught up in a moment of stress and, before I could stop myself, I would be listening to the NAG. Don't worry if that happens to you. I realized that after years of habitual listening to my NAG, it wasn't easy to break the addiction. Be patient … take it one step at a time and remember to say, "I am humility."

Shhhhhh … Just Listen, Love and Live!

"I scream and scream, and you're not listening. I need attention and I need it NOW!"

Teresa's Story

Teresa was angry and depressed. She had come into the Goodness Experience with high hopes and enjoyed her first three days of Goodness. (Even though it had taken more than a month to understand and live these first three days of Goodness – "What if?" "I Am Gratitude," and, "I Am Value.") She had problems when it came to humility. She had felt intimidated by others throughout her life. And after discovering her value, she questioned why she was going to have to 'bow down' to others? She was very confused, and I didn't blame her.

I explained to her, "You don't have to see others as domineering, intimidating, or pushing you to do things you don't agree with; and you don't have to sit like an obedient lamb, never speaking and never being heard. Humility is quite the opposite. In fact, this was where your power begins. Humility is the most powerful and potent aspect of love. Your humility is simply listening and acting purely from your Divine Connection."

A few weeks later, she was beaming with happiness when I saw her. She told me about being in a sales meeting with her boss where, as usual, he was shouting her down, insisting that she do something his way. She listened to her Divine Connection rather than reacting. As he ranted and railed, she sat and listened quietly. Her Divine Connection prompted her to listen to what his heart was saying to her in the midst of his ranting. She stayed calm and receptive. She was listening for the 'right solution.' In this situation, the words came to her as though she was reading them from her heart. She was able to soothe the situation through the humility of responding to her Divine Connection. She discovered that in a potentially explosive situation, she could maintain her poise and retain her power.

For Teresa, the nicest part about learning to practice humility was that it carried over to her clients, her sales increased and she became salesperson of the year. Humility allowed her to give effortlessly.

Larry's Story

Larry was a single father with a 13-year-old daughter, a beautiful girl. Needless to say, boys were after her night and day. Larry was also a police officer and accustomed to handling situations in the form of rules, law and order. He had found this method helpful in his line of work, but with his daughter it seemed to rupture every situation.

Larry came to a Goodness Experience Introductory Seminar on a dare ... by his daughter. A friend of hers had been battling with her mother who had attended a Goodness Experience Introduction and later taken the Goodness Workshop. The mother-daughter conflict had been resolved by learning the power of Goodness and practicing its principles.

Larry thought in the beginning that Goodness was nothing more than 'Pollyanna gibberish.' That was until a bitter fight erupted between him and his daughter.

In the midst of the harsh words he was barking out at her, he stopped. He closed his eyes and thought about how much he loved his daughter and how much he would love to share with her that love; rather than always being the one who had to be the 'bad guy.'

What if, he thought, my daughter and I could get along and work out our differences without the drama of anger?

When he began to speak again, the tone of his voice changed, and he poured out to her all the things he wanted for her; how much he knew she had suffered from not having a mother. He admitted he was probably over-protective. At this point, they began to communicate and allow their relationship to express humility by listening to one another. They were communicating through their highest sense of who they were. Together they healed the scars from the past, and their relationship took on harmony and compassion in understanding one another.

Kimberly's Story

Kimberly had a disagreement with a friend. It was a struggle between two willful women. It was one of those 'cat fights' when both women were stressed and out of sorts, and the turmoil that developed between them had escalated to the point they no longer spoke to one another. Kimberly felt completely justified, and her friend felt the same.

I asked her this "What if?" "Could you and your friend re-establish your friendship? What would you want your friend to do to free her from the anger?"

She answered, "Just a kind word. I don't even want an apology. I think we just had a terrible misunderstanding."

"Well, think about it, and dismiss the anger you feel about your friend. Dismiss it completely – don't give it a place to live and breathe. Don't do what the NAG wants. Instead practice humility."

Kimberly said that she would work on it. Several weeks later, she called to say she had called her friend and invited her for coffee. Her friend had been a little aloof in the beginning. Kimberly very honestly told her she missed her friendship and she knew their disagreement could be resolved.

They both started recalling better times in their friendship and both were laughing as they finished their coffee. By the time they got up to leave, they were making plans to go shopping.

There are countless instances in the Goodness of our lives when we can simply dismiss anger, resentment and hurt. Humility is your power in resolving the Nag's misery, and this recognition brings respect, trust and understanding for yourself and others.

The companion to humility is accepting the contentment it brings: "All needs are met now."

Activating Humility

- List a fear: _____
- Take a deep breath.
- Pause.
- Listen.
- Think of a loving moment. For example: 'I fear I am losing my home." Pause, take a deep breath, listen and think: "How do I feel when I see a child smile?"
- See and feel the fear disappear.

Think humility. Love is all around. I can see it; I can feel it; I can be it. I am never without a home. Love is as effortless as a child's smile; or the most romantic moment with your boyfriend/husband/companion/spouse.

_____

_____

_____

_____

_____

_____

_____

_____

_____

_____

GOODNESS NOTES

I'm listening ... can you hear me?

_____

_____

_____

_____

_____

_____

_____

_____

_____

_____

_____

_____

_____

_____

_____

_____

_____

_____

_____

_____

_____

_____

_____

_____

_____

_____

GOODNESS NOTES

I'm loving ... can you feel me?

_____

_____

_____

_____

_____

_____

_____

_____

_____

_____

_____

_____

_____

_____

_____

_____

_____

_____

_____

_____

_____

_____

GOODNESS NOTES

I'm living ... can you see me?

_____

_____

_____

_____

_____

_____

_____

_____

_____

_____

_____

_____

_____

_____

_____

_____

_____

_____

_____

_____

_____

_____

_____

_____

" 'I'm this! I'm that!' You'll never be good enough."

DAY 5:   I Am Beautiful

Goodness Purpose

- Focus on your unique-i-city which unifies our diversity.
- Understand your beauty.
- What's on the inside shows on the outside. It's the mirror of your soul.

Goodness Action

- Express your beauty.
- When you talk to anyone today, say your words with kindness, gentleness, care and compassion. This is the recipe for beauty.
- When you walk today, think creatively. Think of fireflies dancing, shining and being, and how effortlessly they reflect beauty.
- With every thought, see beauty in every motion and in every image. If your thoughts are from beauty, your life will reflect the power of your 'unique-i-city.' This is the Divine Connection.

"I am the most beautiful woman in the world." I could hardly get the words out, much less feel any truth in that statement. I knew I yearned inside to be beautiful. I wanted to see beauty everywhere. I wanted to experience beauty in every moment, to bask in the beauty of life. An 'impossible dream'? I had always thought this would remain a 'dream' and was definitely outside of any reality for me ... until I discovered a new way of seeing, experiencing and being beautiful.

The Nag Knew Better ... or So She Thought!

I walked to the mirror and all I saw were sags, wrinkles, too much weight, too little muscle tone – imperfection after imperfection. I tried on a dress from last season and the cleaners had 'shrunk' it. Nice try! Or maybe, more honestly, I'd just had a few too many dishes of ice cream. I sat down on the edge of the bed and sighed. The NAG was right; I would never be beautiful.

I wondered if I should look into plastic surgery. They could suck the fat right out of my thighs and stomach; tighten my face, give me high cheekbones and make me beautiful. I thought about this for a moment. That would make me look better but I wanted to take it a step further; I wanted to feel from the inside first. *I am beautiful! Now!*

I knew that looking beautiful on the outside was at the beck-and-call of fad and fashion. I wanted more; I wanted to feel a beauty that transcended time and fads. I didn't want to look like anyone else. I wanted to see and express my own unique and un-matched beauty. I had been learning that I was unique and origi-nal in every way and I needed to see this in myself.

We've all heard people say: "Beauty is what's on the inside." Yeah, right! Try telling that handsome guy in the office down-stairs from me, "Beauty is on the inside." He does a double-take when he sees a girl who is a perfect 'ten.' Anyone who says, "Beauty is on the inside" ought to try living in the real world where you're not supposed to eat, but become mannequin-like to find your beauty.

It dawned on me that I was listening to the NAG. This MUD she was throwing at me was not the truth. Aha! I heard my Divine Connection.

What Is Beauty?

Isn't beauty an intangible thing? Is beauty in the eye of the beholder? What is true beauty? I discovered true beauty is always mine; it is who I am. Beauty is my uniqueness. The way I speak, what I say, how I feel. My beauty is my unique expression of me. No one else can duplicate my beauty; this was my divine connection to my heart's desire.

I had to start seeing beauty in everything about myself – from the inside to the outside – with every thought I felt and with every step I took. I had to believe in the things I saw *in* myself, such as humor, poise, love, spontaneity, intelligence, creativity – these qualities were what I needed to learn and honor about myself.

Even if I didn't believe these things right now, I needed to start demanding to see my *unique contribution*. Once I demanded this of myself, I began to see my beauty more clearly.

I also had to stop believing that with every year I was going to lose my beauty. I had to stop believing that the screen star actress I admired was more beautiful than me. Most of all, I had to stop believing what the NAG was saying. I had to look at things through a lens of beauty and discover my own uniqueness as the most beautiful person in the world. I am the original and no one can duplicate what I have to give.

We each have a tremendous opportunity to discover our beautifully unique selves. The only limitation anyone has is their fear of seeing themselves as beautiful, and fear of not measuring up to another. I had to learn that beauty is not a competition, but a real presence in each of us and in everything we do.

I Am Beautiful

Pause. Take time. Recognize throughout the day your unique and precious beauty, your Goodness and your heart's desire. Honor these qualities, respect these qualities and you will shine in resplendent beauty. When you have lost that sense of beauty, stop, listen and ask to see your beauty ... *your* Divine Connection will show you the way.

Our unique beauty is a posture that projects toward the world – a posture that takes courage, desire and persistence.

Just remember these lyrics by Joe Cocker: "You Are So Beautiful to Me ...." Your Divine Connection says it to you everyday in every way.

Normally, we would include several case stories at this point, but the following letter spoke on so many levels about beauty, we felt we needed to run it in its entirety.

Phlorene's Story ... In Her Own Words

I had a very, very hard time with "I am beauty." Many things in my personal life were crashing down around me and I was supposed to be thinking: "I am beauty."

Give me a break, I thought several times. Who the hell has time to be beautiful while fighting 'snakes in the grass'?

But, I kept going back to it, over and over and over again. Something about this would not let me go. And I knew, unless I understood this lesson, I would not be able to move on.

I was just not getting how one could 'be' beautiful without actually 'being beautiful or feeling beautiful.' In other words, I thought it was a physical thing. Never thinking of myself as being beautiful, I just wasn't getting it.

And then I went back to the source: the actual definition of beauty: "pleasing to the senses." Note the plural. Beauty is in sight, sound, feeling, thoughts, emotion. It's not just and sometimes not ever a physical thing. I finally realized that everyone can be and is beauty; it has nothing to do with actual physical beauty. One is as one does and thinks and acts.

A kind word and/or deed, a genuine smile, meeting anger from another person with kindness; patience, graciousness. All of those things represent beauty. Beauty comes from within, not from without. Beauty is as beauty does, thinks, responds, behaves. Finally, after many, many months, I Got It! It is being beautiful that makes us beautiful.

Even the most beautiful person can behave ugly and therefore be thought of as ugly, and even the most awful looking person can behave beautifully and be thought beautiful.

I went back and forth on this so many times and realized I had confused inner beauty with physical beauty for so long I'd closed myself off to others. My bedroom window, for instance, for years and years has had not only alumi-num foil on it, but cardboard and duct tape, as well. I didn't want anyone looking at me and I didn't want to be seeing anyone or anything.

Well, after it hit me that our actions and thoughts are what manifest themselves as beauty, I took all the layers of stuff off my window that I thought made me 'invisible,' which is what I'd wanted to be for so long. I finally let 'light' in, and I liked it.

I started really listening and paying attention to how I spoke, acted, talked, walked, even paying attention to my handwriting, as well as my thoughts about others. And many lessons came to me during this period. The old adage:

"Judge not, lest ye be judged," the Golden rule: "Do unto others as you would have them do unto you," "Act, don't react," etc., thinking about children and how precious they are, how simple and beautiful they are, no matter what they look like. And my father's words to me time and time again: "Hurry slowly."

"I am beautiful" really hit me hard once I finally realized what we were talking about. I noticed more kindness from others, such as when, one day shortly after I finally understood this lesson, a young man pulled up next to me at a stop light. Although he was in a 'low rider,' had numerous tattoos and piercings, and looked disheveled, he was actually very nice. He asked me if he could pull in front of me as he had to make a left turn up ahead. He said he didn't want to just 'floor it' and race in front of me.

I was stunned and, of course, said yes, and told him how much I appreciated him asking rather than pulling in front of me, cutting me off and perhaps causing an accident. I also realized that if I'd judged him by his looks, I would have been suspicious, probably ignoring him, thinking that he was just wanting money or something, or immediately distrusting him because he was not 'beautiful' to look at. One certainly would not have thought him beautiful ... but he is.

Then, a few days later, while sitting in a movie theatre with a friend, two women went to sit down in front of us. One of them turned around before taking her seat and asked me, "Do you mind if we sit here? I don't want my head to be in your way." Again I was speechless. Someone was actually concerned about being in someone's way at a movie theatre. Of course, I told her I appreciated her asking me, but no, she would not be in my way.

(Now I ask you, when has that ever happened; someone actually being concerned that they might inconvenience you?)

Everything suddenly became more beautiful. The trees, flowers, people, things...

I had cataracts removed during this time as well, and I couldn't help wonder if any part of that was emotional, from not wanting to 'see' or 'be seen.'

For years, I had been going too far the other way, speaking the truth, even if it was hurtful to someone, rather than being me – the person who saw beauty and purpose in everyone. Impatient; impractical. Wanting to be invisible.

'I am beautiful' was the toughest lesson yet, but now I have it, and it is really mine to keep. I have noticed so much about so many things since I learned this lesson.

Thank you, Janice, for helping me to 'see' again.

"What's the big deal about beauty?"

Activating Beauty
List the beauty within your day:

_____

_____

_____

_____

GOODNESS NOTES

Your Beauty is everywhere you look.

_____

_____

_____

_____

_____

_____

_____

_____

_____

_____

_____

_____

_____

_____

_____

_____

_____

_____

_____

_____

_____

GOODNESS NOTES

Everywhere you look is *your* Beauty.

_____

_____

_____

_____

_____

_____

_____

_____

_____

_____

_____

_____

_____

_____

_____

_____

_____

_____

_____

_____

_____

_____

_____

_____

_____

_____

GOODNESS NOTES

Your Beauty is constant.

_____

_____

_____

_____

_____

_____

_____

_____

_____

_____

_____

_____

_____

_____

_____

_____

_____

_____

_____

_____

_____

_____

DAY 6:   I Am Love

Goodness Purpose

- Spiritually erase scars from the past.
- Dissolve your anger.
- Love is everywhere you are.

Goodness Action

- For 24 hours, stop any fearful, angry, hateful thoughts.
- If an unloving thought creeps into your mind and you act on it, *reverse it!* This gives NAG-i-tivity zero power to enter your life.
- If you say something unloving, *reverse it* and make a loving statement. Please don't just say, "I'm sorry," and leave it at that. Re-stating an unloving thought with a loving one *is* the activity of Goodness. It changes what you feel in your heart and allows your Goodness to shine by loving yourself enough to erase all NAG-i-tivity.

I thought this would be the easiest day I would have in discovering my Goodness Experience. *Love,* I thought, *is the most natural thing in the world.* Love is my heartbeat, the enriching life force that I wanted to feel and experience each day. As I began my day, thinking about love, expressing love, receiving love, luxuriating in love, I realized there were a lot of moments in that day when I wasn't embracing, feeling or seeing love.

I was afraid to release my fears and love all things, all the time. What if my love was misplaced? Or, worse yet, rejected? Do I love only to get what I want?

As I delved deeper in uncovering my fears, I asked other daunting questions: *Is my heart frozen? Am I capable of loving? Are the past scars too painful to allow me the freedom I want — to love unconditionally? To love unconditionally means I have to love myself and others by this same standard.* This was a real eye-opener. That's when I discovered a 3-step process:

1.   I realized I first had to learn to love *myself* unconditionally. When I thought of this, I cringed. How could I ever love myself unconditionally?

2.   It takes forgiveness. I had to release every angry recrimination and judgment I had about myself and others. I learned for every fault I saw, I had to let it go, allow and learn to express my Goodness.

3.   Accept Goodness. I couldn't carry the burden of blame or guilt, I had to let go of anger and practice forgiveness.

I learned through my Divine Connection that I could not tie others' opinion (good or bad) to my success. I needed to accept that I was always the expression of love.

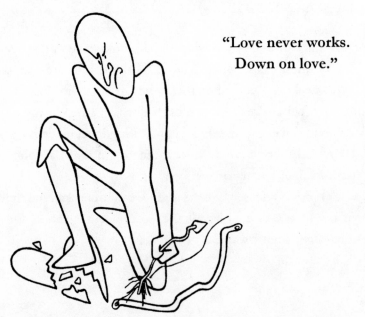

**"Love never works.
Down on love."**

The Nag ... Nagged

"You don't love your job," the NAG echoed in my mind as I drove to work. "You got angry at your daughter last night because you lost patience." I could hear the NAG laughing. I had faltered and she was right. The NAG ranted, "You and your whims. *'I am love, I am gratitude.'* Hah! Be smart and get with the program. Do unto others before they do unto you. That's my kind of world. Stay on top of the game and don't give anyone the opportunity to hurt you. If you hurt someone's feelings with your words, they'll learn to respect you. Isn't respect a form of intimidation? Stay numb. That's the only way you can keep the world from getting you down."

I hated what the NAG was saying, but I also wondered if she was right. Was I willing to risk my heart? Was I willing to look in the face of crisis and demand to see love rather than turmoil? How stupid would that be? Yet, if my heart yearned to love, to be free, to live more fully, to laugh more freely, to love more deeply, how could I be harmed? Was I going to be a leader in my own life or was I going to cower to the NAG?

I made the choice; I was going to be a leader.

Love — It's a Habit

I realized if love was to become a habit, I had to quit blaming others — including myself — when I didn't feel loved or loving, or when I got angry. The NAG had a funny way of turning things around and making me the victim and 'them' the predators.

I made a list of past hurts, traumas, problems, and difficulties. My list became a long list of scars on the landscape of my life. I thought about them. I re-assessed them. Could I find a glimmer of hope and love in these events? I started to see how each agonizing experience had also made a positive contribution to my life.

I recognized no one is really a victim. We make our choices and then try to blame someone else for the results if they are bad. Everyone has a justified excuse to see themselves as a victim; and what good does that do?

I wanted to see myself as a leader. Leaders are born out of how they deal with crisis, not how they justify if there is no answer. I wanted to listen to my Divine Connection and resolve my problems in relationships, my work, and my financial difficulties.

My LOVE exercise began by discovering the treasure of transforming each un-loving experience to a loving one. I cherished this list, once I had changed my perspective.

Now it's your turn. Make a list. Start living love.

Example:

Unloving Experience: My husband and I had a bitter argument that led to divorce.

Treasure: I had to realize and listen to my Divine Connection that was always giving Goodness to me. I had to see my husband in a Goodness light. This freed me from anger, hate and recrimination. By giving and receiving love unconditionally, I found I could never be touched by those NAG-i-tive thoughts, and this manifested into a material presence of harmony. The divorce took place, and opened an entirely new and happier life for me.

Unloving Experience:
Lost all my money
Lost my home

Treasure:
I was always supplied
Love is abundant
I have the experiences and the
knowledge my home is always
with me. No B.S. – it's the Truth.
I choose my new home freely!

Unloving Experience:

Treasure:

_____

_____

_____

_____

_____

_____

_____

_____

**"I am too cool to be sucked into
that love stuff! Try making love
pay the bills."**

Marcia's Story

Marcia was a very talented writer, a very beautiful woman, but she had little patience with the world. She learned on her journey of "I am love" that this four-letter word was elusive ... and much more complex than she had led herself to believe. When she thought of love, she believed this feeling was always warm, soft and beautiful.

But why wasn't this feeling working in her relationships? She didn't love the outside world at all. In fact, she would rather stay home than be around people who bored her.

I asked her, "Why are you afraid?"

The question was a shock to her. "I'm not afraid of anything," she answered.

"Are you sure?"

She looked at me with confusion. She had been in the Goodness workshop long enough to know that there was something she was missing about "I am love." I said, "Love is more than being around only those you like. Love is everywhere, and if you don't see love, then you don't know love. You've never experienced the deepest love and you have never given your best in love."

She looked as though she was going to cry, or perhaps throw the nearest vase at me.

I went on, "Love is to cease resisting Good. This is what the Bible teaches, the prophets, the wise thinkers of our time. Love is simple and love is complex, but it is always with us, and within us."

She resisted what I was saying, but two weeks later she returned. "I had a run-in with my ex-husband." (Her divorce had been in the headlines and had been a very bitter time in her life.) "My first thought when I saw him was anger. I looked at him and made a snide remark. He responded with his own barb. Then the thought came to me – 'I am love.' I felt the warmth of that feeling as I was standing in front of him, not because I was still in love with him, or had any residual feelings from our relationship. It was a recognition of who I was. 'I am love' kept pounding in my head. I looked up at him and smiled because I knew 'I am love.' It wasn't loving him or finding love in return. It was love – I was love – from the tip of my toes to the top of my head.

"He smiled back at me. We looked at one another and we both knew there was no more anger or hatred. Maybe, we were both love."

Sandra's Story

Sandra lived life 'in the fast lane,' never taking time to settle down, find enduring relationships or even establish a sense of home. She was always on the run, going from one lifestyle to another, until she met a man who completely captivated her.

Sandra was having a hard time accepting a 'real' relationship. Her life had been a series of 'one-night stands,' sport sex as I call it. She had never stopped to think of love or herself as "I am love." She couldn't trust others to give her love. Sandra had come from a family of wealth who gave her money, but not much else. Both her parents were busy and on the run in their own lives, and she was left with a series of others to raise her into adulthood. Sandra had never developed anything other than surface relationships.

When Sandra heard the words 'love more deeply' in the early introduction of the Goodness Experience, it had struck a chord. She thought of her new relationship with a man with whom she did want a deeper relationship.

But ...

Sandra had no patience to experience this kind of love.

I talked to her about the fears that go along with intimacy, and how loving more deeply is learning to overcome those fears with knowing "I am love."

Suddenly, Sandra's fears poured out in tears. She sobbed as she re-played the 'hurts' of her sport sex adventures. She had always wanted to listen to her heart, and yet when she did, there was emotional pain to reckon with. She had built up a wall that would not allow her to experience intimacy, only physical sensation.

I encouraged her to listen to her heart, and learn to love unconditionally – step by step. I knew it wouldn't happen overnight, and explained, "You might take one step forward and two steps backward, but if you listen to your Divine Connection, you will not only find the way to love more deeply, but it will be the most satisfying experience you have ever known."

She had to learn "I am love" is trusting yourself first, and having the courage to love with abandon – without fear.

Several months later, I went to her wedding and, before she threw her bouquet, she told me she hoped whoever caught it would take the 'Goodness Experience' seminars and learn that intimacy and love are only found through understanding the power of Goodness.

Activating Love:
Open your heart and touch your world with love.

(Examples:

Smile for no reason at all.

Bless an enemy.

Laugh out loud.

Kiss your reflection.

Tell someone nice things you *love* about your life.

GOODNESS NOTES

"Love ... Love ... Love ... Love is all you need."

— The Beatles

_____

_____

_____

_____

_____

_____

_____

_____

_____

_____

_____

_____

_____

_____

_____

_____

_____

_____

_____

_____

_____

_____

_____

_____

GOODNESS NOTES

"Love me tender." — Elvis Presley

_____

_____

_____

_____

_____

_____

_____

_____

_____

_____

_____

_____

_____

_____

_____

_____

_____

_____

_____

_____

_____

GOODNESS NOTES

LOVE is how you say it:

I love you
Ek het jou lief
Te dua
Ana behibak
Ana behibek
Yes kez sirumen
M'bi fe
Ami tomake bholobashi
Ya tabe kahayu
Nahigugma ako kanimo
Obichom te
Soro, lohn nhee ah
Ngo oiy ney a
T'estimo
Tsi ge yu i
Ne mohotatse
Ndimakukonda
Ti tenqu caru
Mi aime jou
Volim te
Miluji te
Jeq Elsker big
Ik hou van jou
Amin mela Ile
Mi amas vin
Ma armastan sind
Afgreki'
Eg elski teg
Doset daram
Mahal kita
Mina rakastan simua
Je t'aime
Je t'adore
Ik hald fan dy
To gra agarn art
Mikvarhar
Ich liebe dich
S'agapo
Hoo thunay prem karoo
choo
Palanggo ko ikaw

Aloha Au Ia'oe
ani ohey otcha
Ohevet ot'cha
Guina higugma ko ikaw
Hum Tumhe Pyar Karte
hoe
Kuv hlub koj
Nu' umi unangwa'to
Szeretiek
Eg elska tig
Palongga ka ikaw
Saya cinta padamu
Negligevapse
Taim i' ngro leat
Ti amo
Aishiteru
Naanu ninna
preetisuttene
Kaluguran daka
Nakupenda
Tu magel moga cha
Sarang Heyo
Te amo
Es tevi miilu
Bahibak
Tave myliu
Ech hun dech gaer
Te Sakam
Saya cintakan mu
Aku cinta padamu
Njan Ninne
Premikunnu
Inhobbok
Wo ai ni
Me tula prem karto
Kanbhik
Ana moajaba bik
Ni mits neki
Ayor anosh'ni
Jeg Elsker Deg
Syota no kitall

Inaru Taka
Mi ta stimabo
Dao-set daaram
Iay ovlay ouyay
Kocham Ciebie
Eu te amo
Te iubesc
Ya tebya liubliu
Tha gra\dh agam art
Volim te
Ke a go rata
Maa takhe pyar kendo
ahyan
Techihhila
Lu'bim ta
Ljubim te
Te quiero
Te amo
Ninapenda wewe
Jag alskar dig
Ich lieb Di
Mi lobi joe
Mahal kita
Wa go ei li
Ua Here Vau la Oe
Nan unnai
katholikaraen
Nenu ninnu
premistunnanu
Chan rak khun
Phom rak khun
Seni Seyiyorum
Ya tebe kahayu
mai oap say pyaor karta
hoo
Anh ye^u em
Em ye^u anh
'Rwy'n dy garu di
Ikh hob dikh
Ma ni fe

"See how far love will
get you."

"What am I going to do
now? She's in love with
everyone!"

DAY 7:   **I Am ME!**

Goodness Purpose

- Accept ME—Accept everyone!
- Love ME—Love everyone!
- Express ME—Express everyone!

Goodness Action

- Dance at least one dance today, even if it's in your living room by yourself. Or with your dog or cat.
- Smile at least 10 times at someone who is a stranger
- Kiss the one you love.

By the end of this first week, I had developed a new attitude. I was timidly beginning to start my day differently. Before I got up in the morning, I would stop and remember who I was. Each morning before I put one foot out of bed, I mentally listed my many reasons for gratitude, value, humility, beauty, and love. I rose to meet my day without fear and worked to maintain that posture throughout the day and into the night, with a sense of purpose beyond just getting through the hours. I consciously became aware of these qualities in myself and others.

I wanted to be ME ... the best me I could be. I *lived* through my new knowledge – I didn't just exist.

Life is what you make it. *"If God is the DJ, life is the dance floor, love is the rhythm, you are the music. Get your ass on the dance floor!"*
                                                            —Pink

Now live your day that is unfolding all the Goodness there is in the world. Get on the dance floor. *BE YOU!*

Activating "Me":

Be extraordinary today

GOODNESS NOTES

I *am* Great ... I *am* Marvelous ... I *am* Magnificent!

_____

_____

_____

_____

_____

_____

_____

_____

_____

_____

_____

_____

_____

_____

_____

_____

_____

_____

_____

_____

_____

_____

_____

_____

GOODNESS NOTES

I am Lovely!

GOODNESS NOTES

I am Beautiful!

_____

_____

_____

_____

_____

_____

_____

_____

_____

_____

_____

_____

_____

_____

_____

_____

_____

_____

_____

_____

_____

_____

_____

_____

WEEK TWO: ALLOW GOODNESS

To allow is a willingness to grow and change ... for the better.
Allow your *Goodness qualities* to emerge, expand and enhance
every moment of your life. Allow yourself to grow and evolve
into your divinely designed uniqueness.

DAY 8: Overcoming Fear of Change and Living the Promise

Today write down all of the doubts and fears you feel about yourself and your life. Don't hold back. Say anything and everything that causes fear for you. And as you list these inadequacies you feel, ask the question, "Are these real?" Remember the NAG builds up these false fears in our mind.

Next ...

Ask yourself, "Can I overcome whatever I doubt or fear?" If you answer, "Yes, I can," you are allowing the truth and Goodness in your life to take center stage.

Doubt comes from a belief of not belonging, not fitting into the world, a belief of being mismatched in a world that sometimes feels foreign. Overcoming doubt and fear demands seeing what phantoms of fear chase you through life, and these fears need to be written down and *dismissed as cruel little culprits*.

The first time I accomplished this, my stomach turned flip-flops. I doubted my ability to speak in front of people and avoided situations that might develop into speaking without a script. I dug deep to find out why I was so fearful of this experience. What if I stumbled over my words? What if I completely forgot what I was going to say? What if I went brain dead and had nothing to say? By the time I'd finished magnifying my inability, I doubted my ability to even put a sentence together. It was a silly fear, but it was limiting and influencing my life, and needed to be overcome.

I had to see this was a ridiculous doubt. I talked on the phone, didn't I? I wrote letters, didn't I? I could memorize a script and speak ... aha! I realized that when I was able to speak comfortably, I was behind something – a hidden wall, the telephone line, another character – but it wasn't me out in front of a group of people. I found protection through the faceless words of a letter.

It all had to do with self-esteem. Back to the beginning, I looked at the Goodness qualities I had learned about – gratitude, humility, love, value, and "What if?"

I took the time to appreciate what I'd already discovered about myself, and listened to my heart's desire. I wanted to overcome my fear and grow and change.

Then I remembered my Divine Connection and stopped listening to the NAG. I listened, awakened and lived the Goodness Experience. I knew myself to be a woman who was created from the very beginning of existence by a Law of beauty, graciousness, and intelligence. The woman I wanted to be – the woman I was.

I thought about the many qualities I could express if I was listening to my heart – graciousness, kindness, intelligence, beauty, humor, confidence, humility. These were the qualities I wanted to feel when I stood up to speak.

I went to work thinking about what those things meant, how they looked, and how they felt. It took time and I had to let go of past images and pay attention to the NAG-i-tive beliefs I was harboring.

I replaced fear and doubt with *spiritual poise*, a phrase that meant I was listening to my Divine Connection; knowing and trusting it. I disconnected from every negative thought about myself. Nothing could happen on the outside until I felt it on the inside. As I held on to this *spiritual poise,* I began to see myself expressing those qualities I had listed earlier. I realized there was a universal Law of Good to support our quest for a better life. A way of being that makes us aware of the Good in our life that is always present. I had to consciously make a choice to either honor the qualities that were already mine or make a NAG-i-tive choice to doubt.

I wanted nothing to do with doubt, so each morning, I consciously made the decision to make the right choice.

As you open your heart to a more purposeful and positive life, you will develop the wisdom and confidence to release your Misery – Uncertainty – Doubt. Misery is made up of past accumulations of doubt – remember the MUD? It's the stuff the NAG leaves to clutter our mental homes. It clouds our thinking, slows us down and makes us want to quit, stay under the covers and never take a step outside our door. When this happens, disconnect and reboot into the Goodness experience.

With each new day, I learned to rise above the power I had given to the NAG – Neurotic Anxiety-ridden Grinch – and her inner voice of doom and gloom that persistently tried to keep me upset and down.

This new focus brought an ordinary life into an extraordinary Goodness Experience. Now isn't that the life you've always wanted to enjoy? The beautiful part is this life you yearn for is tailor-made, exclusively for you, born from your own uniqueness. It's yours to create and experience. It is what is waiting to be exposed.

Now let's get your doubts and fears into the open. Make your list, and begin your three-step process to overcome the fear of change. Let the unknown become your adventure.

Exercise

List anything you fear. Write down every worry, every self-doubt you have, even if it feels silly. Now come on – honesty is the only way. Even if you're 'a-skared' of spiders, put it on the list. Then, in your second step of this exercise, disconnect totally from each fearful thought. Use your spiritual poise to step into the Goodness, and experience the promise.

Your Nag (Fear), Disconnect, Reboot Promise:

Fear	Disconnect	Reboot
Example:	**Reboot:**	**Promise:**
I'm not pretty	I am Beauty	Complete Harmony
I'm not smart	I am Intelligence	Wisdom
_____	_____	_____
_____	_____	_____
_____	_____	_____
_____	_____	_____
_____	_____	_____
_____	_____	_____
_____	_____	_____
_____	_____	_____
_____	_____	_____
_____	_____	_____
_____	_____	_____
_____	_____	_____

Accept the Truth and Release the Lie.

A Lesson from a Pro

I was sitting flipping the channels one afternoon when the phone rang. Later, I came back to the TV screen and saw a handsome man talking, so I turned up the volume. It was Steve Young, former quarterback for the San Francisco 49ers, a man of legendary talent, honored and perceived to be one of the greatest players in football.

"I was afraid," he said. "I was afraid of everything when I was a kid. I was afraid to go to school, afraid to leave my house. The first time I had ever spent the night away from home was my first year in college."

I was dumbstruck – even the great Steve Young had a NAG. I continued to listen as he attributed overcoming his fears to sports. He found his courage, his strength and his spirit of excellence. I saw this truth from his life as overcoming his direst fears with love. He loved football, and that had given him the courage to dismiss his fears.

I knew from my own experience, with love anything is possible. The Bible has been saying this for generations. Great thinkers have said this, and every successful person echoes this thought throughout time, eras, generations, and NOW.

The NAG would say, "Love won't pay the bills." I say, "Yes, it does!"

GOODNESS NOTES

"Do one thing everyday that scares you." — Eleanor Roosevelt

_____

_____

_____

_____

_____

_____

_____

_____

_____

_____

_____

_____

_____

_____

_____

_____

_____

_____

_____

_____

GOODNESS NOTES

"Has fear ever held a man back from anything he really wanted, or a woman either?" — George Bernard Shaw

_____

_____

_____

_____

_____

_____

_____

_____

_____

_____

_____

_____

_____

_____

_____

_____

_____

_____

_____

_____

_____

_____

_____

_____

_____

GOODNESS NOTES

"Before the beginning of great brilliance, there must be chaos.
Before a brilliant person begins something great, they must look
foolish in the crowd." — I Ching

"Help, she's scaring me!"

"I'm afraid."

DAY 9: The Tapestry of a Life

Today and every day is an unfoldment of creation. We create our day through our thoughts, our wishes, our desires. They become our colors, lines, forms and shapes that weave the tapestry of our life. Each day is a new and vibrant design reflecting your consciousness.

Take a deep breath and imagine a clear light from the sky coming straight down from above, illuminating your thoughts, enhancing your wishes, igniting your desires. Feel all the warmth and love of the universe spreading throughout your body, making you feel alive. Each thought is your thread. Each wish is your layer of color. Each desire is a design of love that embraces every event and person in your life.

Some people may look at this and think, "This is really out in la-la land." It's not. If you want to experience only Good in your life, you must allow this Goodness to take form from the warmth and love of this creation power.

So, here are some exercises:

Exercise One:

Write down 20 things you would like to experience in your life, things you desire and felt you never received. (This will negate the unrequited want.)

1 _____

2 _____

3 _____

4 _____

5 _____

6 _____

7 _____

8 _____

9 _____

10 _____

11 _____

12 _____

13 _____

14 _____

15 _____

16 _____

17 _____

18 _____

19 _____

20 _____

NOW pick ten of those things you want to experience more than anything in the world.

1 _____

2 _____

3 _____

4 _____

5 _____

6 _____

7 _____

8 _____

9 _____

10 _____

Now out of those ten, pick five that you want the most.

1 _____

2 _____

3 _____

4 _____

5 _____

Now pick three. Pick the ones that make your heart sing.

1 _____

2 _____

3 _____

Take this piece of paper, fold it and put it in your wallet. Today, take a short walk and think about your three desires. Use your imagination. Experience what you feel. Stop your mind from racing in fear. Stop being snagged by the NAG. Feel the lushness in the tapestry of your Goodness Experience.

Feel it ... languish in it ... and joy in it.

Exercise Two:

When you create from Goodness, you never feel fearful or deprived. Most of us have a feeling of being deprived of something. Our father neglected us; some past boyfriend/girlfriend rejected us … the list goes on. We end up approaching situations from a foundation of fear and want. But, when the tapestry of your life comes from the source of your Divine Connection, you are supplied with an abundance that gives you a positive and rich foundation. When you allow and accept this source to fuel your ability, it totally obliterates any feeling of ever being deprived.

How can you feel deprived if every need is met? All needs are met when we identify with our Goodness. You will feel rich and generous regardless of what your bank account balance says, what model of car you drive, or whether you shop in a thrift store or wear haute couture.

No one can take away the security and warmth of knowing that every need is met with love. Already. Now. The NOW is complete. Exercise that feeling. Watch all the lines and colors of the tapestry of your life blend together, weaving your seamless purpose in the world.

Rest in this beautiful tapestry that is uniquely yours.

ALLOW.

Whenever I think of a tapestry, I see only beauty and I feel only warmth. I was once in an Indian market looking at a wall filled with tapestries. An Indian gentleman approached me and asked to help. I said I couldn't decide which one I wanted, and he gave me a reply that made me think.

"You don't pick a tapestry. The tapestry is your mirror of life."

We both stood and looked at each tapestry. Suddenly, one of the tapestries came into distinct focus through the colors I loved, the designs, and the intricate threads blended one into another.

That hanging became more than just beauty – it was the mirror of what I loved in my life.

I hung the tapestry in my bedroom so I could see it when I awoke every morning. It became a gentle reminder of who I was, where I was, the beauty of the world around me, and just exactly how I fit in.

From that time on, I allowed myself to look at life differently.

Exercise Three:

Words are the threads we use to weave beauty into our lives. Practice allowing yourself to treasure what you say and how you say it.

Treasures of the tapestry
(Living words that create actions)

- **Acceptance**: The final step of knowing, doing and being.
- **Allowing**: Opening your heart with a willingness to move forward.
- **Affirmations**: Expressing, seeing and hearing your Divine Connection; acting on inspiration, rather than reacting.
- **Acknowledgement**: Appreciating.
- **Abundance**: Knowing you have all you need regardless of the 'picture.'
- **Awareness**: Ability to understand your feelings and needs along with those around you.
- **Attention**: Focus in the present and living in the NOW.
- **Balance**: Living in harmony
- **Beauty**: The gift of love within.
- **Courage**: Confidence in following your heart.
- **Creativity**: Expression of your heart's desires and experiencing the highest sense of self.

- **Desire**: The inspiration of love that is the rhythm of your heart.
- **Disconnect**: Total abandonment from false fears.
- **Enthusiasm**: Energy from your heart's desire.
- **Expectancy**: Living in the presence of Good.
- **Faith**: Understanding.
- **Fear**: False illusion.
- **Focus**: Magnifying each moment.
- **Forgiveness**: Giving unconditional love. Letting go of the past and living in the NOW.
- **Giving**: It is living.
- **Goals**: Clarifying your desires.
- **Good**: Your identity. Your protection.
- **Gratitude**: Humility that opens your heart and your life to all the Goodness of the Universe.
- **Growth**: Progressing forward.
- **Happiness**: Seeing your unique self worth.
- **Harmony**: A balance between Universal Good and your heart's desire.
- **Health**: A natural state of wholeness.
- **Hearing**: Responding to Goodness.
- **Heart**: The core of your being. The center of your universe.
- **Honesty**: Living your truth.
- **Humility**: Listening to your Divine Connection.
- **Inspiration**: The 'breath' of your heart's desires.
- **Knowing**: Certainty of Goodness; wealth.
- **Laws**: Guideposts to Goodness.
- **Listening**: The language between you and your Divine Connection.
- **Love**: Feeling and living the Goodness Experience.
- **Miracle**: A natural transcending of the obstacles, removal of all limitation; certainty of Good.

- **Need**: Answers to the very best.
- **Now**: The only place you ever will, have, or are living.
- **Obedience**: Living by the laws of Goodness.
- **Opportunity**: The moment of synchronicity.
- **Patience**: The loving element of poise, allowing Goodness to unfold.
- **Poise**: Feeling only Good in your life regardless of what is or seems to be going on.
- **Power**: The action of Goodness – slowly, gently and lovingly.
- **Promise**: Completeness; fulfillment of all Good.
- **Reboot**: Accepting the truth.
- **Responsibility**: Trusting your Goodness.
- **Spirituality**: Your only being.
- **Trust**: Allowing your heart's desire to manifest.
- **Truth**: The only thing that exists.
- **Transformation**: Allowing your mind, body and soul to progress into fulfillment; growing in every moment; a constant.
- **Value**: Assets of Goodness; priceless; honor.
- **Wealth**: Knowing, trusting all needs are met.
- **Watch**: Acceptance of Goodness.
- **You**: Perfection.

"We don't accomplish anything in this world alone ... and whatever happens is the result of the whole tapestry of one's life and all the weavings of individual threads from one to another that creates something."

— Sandra Day O'Connor:

GOODNESS NOTES

COLOR your world ... It's your tapestry.

_____

_____

_____

_____

_____

_____

_____

_____

_____

_____

_____

_____

_____

_____

_____

_____

_____

_____

_____

_____

_____

GOODNESS NOTES

Paint the scene ... It's your tapestry.

_____

_____

_____

_____

_____

_____

_____

_____

_____

_____

_____

_____

_____

_____

_____

_____

_____

_____

_____

_____

_____

_____

_____

_____

GOODNESS NOTES

Touch your Tapestry with a wish from your Soul

_____

_____

_____

_____

_____

_____

_____

_____

_____

_____

_____

_____

_____

_____

_____

_____

_____

_____

_____

_____

_____

_____

_____

_____

DAY 10:   Trust

You already know how it *feels* to have three of your fondest desires come true. Now, we're going to learn how to stay with those thoughts and feelings of fulfillment all the time. To do this, you must allow GOOD to continuously flow in your life – and this takes TRUST.

If we don't see Good continuously, we are sabotaging all of our hopes and dreams and keeping them in a stagnated state of unreality. We are not trusting our promise of GOODNESS.

You may think this preposterous, but think again. Most of the time we don't get what we want because of self-sabotage that comes from fear of moving forward; fear of the unknown; and an entire list of other NAG-i-tive fears. The NAG always wants to make you feel you are undeserving. Don't buy her story about you – it's not the truth.

You can stand up to her lies when you develop trust. Learning to trust is like developing a muscle. Repetition ... repetition ... repetition.

Trust is relying on the reality of Good in your life. It is a reliance on integrity, and a confident expectation that your trust is deserved. It goes beyond hope. In fact, it is a certainty of Good that we call a miracle. This is the power to know all Good is possible in your life. It's not something that's almost here or there, but is NOW.

I know this is a radical statement. But, it is the promise that you were given the day you were born according to the universal Law of Good that is always present.

Our difficulties stem from believing the NAG and feeling like one. When you believe the NAG, you unconsciously adjust your life, your choices, and your movements. It's the trick of the NAG and *if* you follow her downward spiral into a NAG-i-tive abyss, you will fail. Remember – what we believe, we will see. What we see is what we believe. One of life's riddles. Do you want to see the NAG or Goodness?

Trust is changing the lens; adjusting our vision to focus on the Good in life instead of dwelling on the obstacles we face in our everyday life. You solve your problems by gagging the NAG and stepping into the Goodness Experience, allowing you to solve a problem through positive influences.

How can you possibly find an answer if you are dwelling on the obstacle, trying to learn something from the NAG-i-tive? You will never see how to get around it, through it, or over it. You will be stuck in the MUD.

In the 90s, we heard the catchphrase: "It's all good." Even if it looked bad, we held onto, "It's all good." Some of us took this to mean, "Grin and bear it," but I think it meant to trust a fact of the universe. It *is* all Good, so let's live it, see it, feel it and KNOW IT!

Trusting will help keep all Goodness in the forefront of consciousness, and this propels you toward your most cherished desires. If you keep this conscious, positive and truthful outlook in your life, you will allow your desires to become realities and dismiss the element of fear. You will keep progressing toward your desires regardless of the NAG's need to stop you.

Let the NAG-i-tive winds blow around you, but keep your spiritual poise and focus on your heart's desire. This is trust.

Trust is valid and worthy as long as you honor who you are – that person who is true and lovable. When you live from the heart and express your heart's qualities, you are lovable and can simply be, experiencing nothing else.

If you feel intimidated or thrown off balance, go back to that feeling of Good flowing from your Divine Connection that is only a thought away. Take a deep breath and feel that beam of warm, assuring life that permeated your being this morning as you awoke to creation's gift, called today.

Remember, you are created to experience your own individual fulfillment in your very own life. You have a divinely designated purpose. It's your show and you are the star, so trust this fact and open your heart to the Goodness that is already yours. Honor your feelings about what you want and how you desire to feel. Believe that you are beautiful and Good. When you do this, the right actions will become apparent in your life. This is a universal law that is ever present.

Become intimately aware of your unique identity, confide in yourself and listen for the answers that this Goodness Experience will supply to you.

Recognize how trust creates progress and has never failed you. List all of the things you've already achieved in your life, all of the things you've wanted and gotten. You'll be amazed at the power you've been expressing every day of your life. When you consciously stay aware of this Goodness, you'll multiply your ability to achieve all Good.

Now look into the past and start your list:

1 _____

2 _____

3 _____

4 _____

5 _____

6 _____

7 _____

8 _____

9 _____

10 _____

(ad infinitum)

(Psst! Say a little 'thank you' and know that every day you have the power to always achieve the greatest Good for yourself and the world around you.)

Trust Your Heart and Soul

"Trust yourself. Create the kind of self that you will be happy to live with all your life. Make the most of yourself by fanning the tiny, inner sparks of possibility into flames of achievement."
— Foster C. McClellan, entrepreneur

"Who can I trust? I can't trust anyone."

"It's dark in here."

GOODNESS NOTES

Trust with all your heart ...

GOODNESS NOTES

Trust with all your mind ...

GOODNESS NOTES

Trust with all your soul!

_____

_____

_____

_____

_____

_____

_____

_____

_____

_____

_____

_____

_____

_____

_____

_____

_____

_____

_____

_____

_____

_____

_____

_____

_____

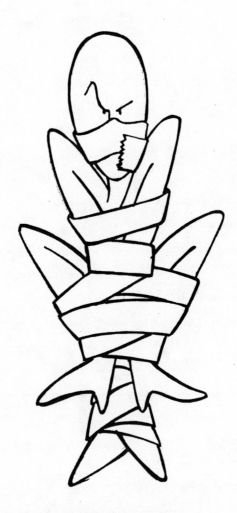

"It's too late. I can't do it."

DAY 11:   Acting on Your Desires

*When you wake up today, **know** you already possess
everything you need to experience a happy and fulfilled
life. (Remember, you live in Goodness)
Yes, there are desires to realize, but today you take the
next step: to understand that your desires are reality,
whether you can see them at the moment or not. Become aware of these possibilities by listening and understanding that all lives are governed by an eternal presence
of Good. And if your motives are Good, your results are
Good.*

I can already hear your NAG: "Isn't that a crock of it?" Well,
that's what the NAG would like you to believe. She wants your
total attention so you can feel bad and experience the worst. But,
whether you are challenged by ten thousand problems today or
just one, you can make the choice to rest and rely on the Laws of
Good. Remember the tapestry of love and fulfillment that seam-
lessly holds your life in Goodness? Some people define this powerful presence as God, Jesus Christ, Allah, Yahweh, Elohim,
Jehovah, etc., but the presence of Good – regardless of how it
comes to you – is the law that governs the universe.

I can hear your response: "What do you mean? I'm frail. I'm
human. I always make mistakes. I'm not good enough. I fall short
of my goals. I want to achieve things but I can't. I don't have
time. It's too late in my life." All of these bellowing complaints
are nothing more than the NAG's excuses. So wipe the MUD off
and get into the Goodness.

Now you have to ask yourself the hard question: "Is it that I
can't or I won't?" Think about it. You may be surprised at what's
stopping you.

As we have discussed before, we make choices every moment of every day. Our choices create our experience. These choices reveal who controls our life – the NAG or our Divine Connection.

One of the things we often forget is *honoring* – honoring our choices, honoring ourselves and honoring our loved ones. We sometimes make knee-jerk responses based on what's going to be the best for others. If we make choices that only appease others, we are not only cheating ourselves, but we are cheating them. Our basis for any action must be the rightness of it.

Sometimes we are afraid to make the choice we want. We make choices that are what we think we *should* want. We don't think through our choices and really try to understand what is right. When we are being influenced by the NAG or our own personal ego, we become confused and feel burned out and discouraged when we don't get our way.

I know how you feel. I have felt too busy and too stressed to take the time to understand the motivations of my choices and to listen and honor my Divine Connection. When I made the wrong choice, I had to question my motives. Was I doing this because of someone else's opinion? Was I doing this because *I* wanted to? The tough question always was, "Am I trying to manipulate and control someone?" or, "Am I trying to guilt them into doing it my way?"

I used to run from this kind of questioning until I realized, to live in the Goodness Experience and to have only Good in my life, I needed to make better choices. My actions had to be purified.

Changing my thoughts to see only Goodness and beauty was not a Pollyanna experience. It was not putting my head in the sand and ignoring the obstacles; it was simply acting on my desire to choose a path of rightness. There were many instances when this was challenging. In the beginning I didn't trust myself, and when I chose to see only Good, I was afraid it wouldn't work out. Then I would bring myself back to the Goodness and trust and rely on those laws. It didn't always work out the way I thought it would. But, day by day, I kept listening and watching and allowing. I began to see my experiences changing; I was learning to live from my heart, learning to discover the *rightness*; and *experiencing fulfillment*.

I was discovering what life was supposed to be, but I had to break the habit of thinking that Good was an illusive dream that could never be mine.

I struggled as I got to know myself as a person who already had all the wonderful qualities I yearned for. Surprisingly, I began to naturally experience beauty, success and harmony in my everyday life. But it took time to learn about the Goodness that had always been with me.

Most of us are so busy focusing on what is wrong in our lives that if the greatest event in the world hit us on the head, we wouldn't see it or experience it or trust it. We wear ourselves out just trying to keep from falling apart, keep our family from falling apart, or keep our spouses from falling apart. It's like a treadmill that never stops – exhausting and depleting. We yearn for sleep when the fact is, we need a wake-up call. Eventually, we become numb and unconscious to our desires, who we truly are, and what we want. Usually all we want is for the world to stop.

I became an expert problem solver; if there wasn't a problem ready to solve, I'd go out of my way to find one, just to prove to myself and the world how good I was at finding answers. I got an adrenalin rush from solving one problem and creating another. Remember, the NAG is always at work. We get into this treadmill experience because we don't believe we can be happy; and even if we could be content, we are terrified of being disappointed or bored.

The Goodness Experience is a radical state of thought that shows us the path to happiness. We don't have to chase it or turn ourselves inside out to find it. We just need to listen to our inner voice (Divine Connection) we know as the truth that guides us.

The voice that keeps us aware of the love already surrounding us. If you don't hear it, you need to quiet the NAG, wipe away your thoughts of doubt and discouragement, and allow your mind to fill with worthy thoughts. In that moment, you can see, feel and experience your desires. The more you see it, the more you will have beauty, warmth, intelligence and integrity.

"We are told never to cross a bridge until we come to it, but this world is owned by men who have 'crossed bridges' in their imagination far ahead of the crowd."

— Unknown author

Bill Gates, Coretta King (Mrs. Martin Luther King), General Sidney Shachnow, President John F. Kennedy, Michael Jordan, 'Babe' Ruth, Gloria Steinham, Deepak Chopra, Mary Baker Eddy, Dr. Christine Northrup, Wayne Dyer, Maya Angelou, Martha Graham, Albert Einstein. Each of these successful men and women has crossed bridges in their mind, far ahead of the crowd. What bridge will *you* cross TODAY?

Exercise:

Today is hands on. When you are dealt a problem, stop and think about a choice you can make that will lead to harmony, not destruction. Find the solution instead of dwelling in the aggravation. Ask yourself hard questions about your motives. Write down how you turned the situation around or how you didn't accomplish your goal. Not accomplishing your goal is not a failure. We all learn from experience and this exercise requires you to take a dramatic step – radical reliance on a Law of Good that you may still be unsure about. Just remember: *it works!* (even if you don't believe it at the moment).

_____

_____

_____

_____

_____

_____

_____

_____

_____

_____

_____

GOODNESS NOTES

Build the bridge ...

_____

_____

_____

_____

_____

_____

_____

_____

_____

_____

_____

_____

_____

_____

_____

_____

_____

_____

_____

_____

_____

_____

_____

_____

GOODNESS NOTES

Stay on the bridge ...

_____

_____

_____

_____

_____

_____

_____

_____

_____

_____

_____

_____

_____

_____

_____

_____

_____

_____

_____

_____

_____

_____

_____

_____

_____

GOODNESS NOTES

Help others to cross the bridge ...

_____

_____

_____

_____

_____

_____

_____

_____

_____

_____

_____

_____

_____

_____

_____

_____

_____

_____

_____

_____

_____

_____

DAY 12:   Goodness Date

Today is the day you take yourself out on a date. You can be as extravagant as you would like, or you don't need to spend a dime. But, rule #1 is to treat *yourself* the way you would treat your most treasured friend. Do what your heart desires and talk to yourself the way you want others to talk to you. Make it a loving experience.

If you only have an hour for your date, take it. If you can find an entire afternoon or day, take it. Listen to your heart's desires and act on those desires, regardless of how whimsical or serious you think they may be. Act on the joy ... smile, laugh, dance, be free.

Have a Goodness Day!
PS: Don't invite the NAG!

"There is no such thing in anyone's life as an unimportant day."
— Alexander Woollcott, from *Inspirational Quotes on Life*

GOODNESS NOTES

The Rainbow's End: LAUGHTER

GOODNESS NOTES

Dance with abandon: FREEDOM

_____
_____
_____
_____
_____
_____
_____
_____
_____
_____
_____
_____
_____
_____
_____
_____
_____
_____
_____
_____
_____
_____
_____
_____
_____

GOODNESS NOTES

Shout out loud: FULFILLMENT

DAY 13:   'Bag the NAG' Day

Today should be a national holiday. This can be the first day of your life without NAG-i-tivity. Take a pen and paper and list your assets, the treasures within your soul. Discover and surprise yourself by monitoring every wonderful thought you have.

Today allow love for yourself, for your peers, and for your life. Your list of **allows** can grow longer than what is here, but these affirmations are a start...

- I allow myself to know I am loved completely and unconditionally – *Feel it in your heart.*
- I allow myself to *accept* all the love that is surrounding me – *Feel it in your heart.*
- I allow myself to *feel* gratitude and inspiration as naturally as I take each breath – *Feel it in your heart.*
- I allow myself to *experience* the Goodness and beauty that comes to me today – *See it and feel it in your heart.*
- I allow myself to *focus* on the Good in every moment, regardless of any turmoil that is going on in the world or my life – that means no ifs, ands or buts (i.e., Bag the Nag) – *Feel it in your heart.*

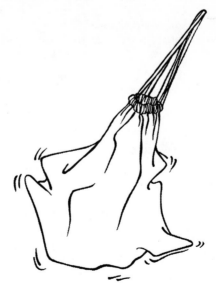

Each one of these affirmations has to do with your thinking. It's not dependent on anyone else or anything else. When you allow yourself to govern your life from the Good coming from your own thoughts, you are able to give more to the world around you. You will be unstoppable. You will see more intelligence, creativity, spontaneity, and love – *everywhere*.

When the NAG tries to stop your Goodness Experience with a, "Yeah, but …" refuse to listen. She's not you. Remember who you are. Today, list your treasure of assets.

If the NAG yells at you about the time you were fired from your job, dismiss that thought with another; what about the time you were promoted in your job, or how relieved you were when you lost that job. Remember, we're always making our own choices – did you really want to keep that job? Or remember when you received a smile from someone you helped that was more rewarding than any payday; or when you had a Good idea used in many ways that helped a company or person.

We spend too much time dwelling on the past, not living in the present and worrying about the future. This is exactly what the NAG wants. Goodness is always NOW and that is the only place you live.

Below are examples of your treasure chest of assets.

What Are Your Assets?

Are you gentle, loving, caring, humble, confident, loyal, open-minded, patient, decisive, assertive, Good-natured, light-hearted, comical, beautiful (inside or outside), generous, optimistic, sweet, sociable, shy, adventurous, reticent, spirited, tolerant, persistent, determined, respectable, accommodating, adaptable, peaceful, cultured, vigorous, unique, empathetic, trustworthy, happy, demonstrative, affectionate, even-tempered, kind, thoughtful, intelligent, balanced, communicative, compassionate, courageous, creative, enthusiastic, faithful, focused, graceful, flexible, responsible, patient, vulnerable, honest, emotionally strong, willing.

Exercise:

- Write a line or more about how you have expressed each one of these qualities.
- Look at the list and on your mental landscape, firmly etch the Good you have accomplished.
- Focus on the Good you express to others and the world around you. The next time the NAG starts to do her number on you, you'll have a treasure chest of protection against her NAG-i-tive barbs.
- Make a list of the qualities in others that you admire. Start working on finding those same attributes within yourself, to be expressed in your own unique way. By appreciating diversity in one another, we find our own individual uniqueness, and each piece fits like a puzzle bringing harmony to our world.
- This journey of discovering your Goodness Experience is individual and all your own. It will not be the same as mine or your best friend's. You are an original and you deserve to see it, live it and enjoy it, with the action of Unique-i-city.

Definition of Unique – (yoo'-nek)...1. one and only, single, sole; 2. having no like or equal, unparalleled; 3. highly unusual, extraordinary, rare, etc.; 4. *a common usage still objected to by some.

—— Daniel Webster (sounds as if Daniel Webster had a NAG)

GOODNESS NOTES

I am unstoppable!

_____

_____

_____

_____

_____

_____

_____

_____

_____

_____

_____

_____

_____

_____

_____

_____

_____

_____

_____

_____

GOODNESS NOTES

I am a thousand kisses!

_____
_____
_____
_____
_____
_____
_____
_____
_____
_____
_____
_____
_____
_____
_____
_____
_____
_____
_____
_____
_____
_____
_____
_____
_____
_____
_____
_____

GOODNESS NOTES

I am a bundle of love!

_____

_____

_____

_____

_____

_____

_____

_____

_____

_____

_____

_____

_____

_____

_____

_____

_____

_____

_____

_____

_____

_____

_____

DAY 14:   Living from Your Heart

It's time to take a stand for what we want to **allow** in our lives.

Do you love what you're doing? Where you're living? How you are living your days? Do you even take the time to think about it?

Some of us are so overwhelmed with responsibilities that we don't take the time to think about whether or not we love ourselves, those around us, and much less what we are doing at the moment. Life is nothing more than a whirlwind of activity that 'whooshes' us from the time we wake up until we lay our head back down on our pillow without the energy to move.

We also use all of this activity as a protection: if we stop juggling our activities, is our world going to fall apart? What would happen if you took time in the morning to think about your day and how you want it to feel as it unfolds? Sca-a-a-a-ry! Don't we just have to take it as it comes?

No! You have control over every moment of the day. Not by rigid fear, but by *allowing* and *accepting* only Good.

Loving who we are and what we do assures us that we can make the choices in our life freely without being forced into a situation of choosing the best of bad worlds. When we don't love what we do in a profession or in our everyday life, we find ourselves putting off the things that we *would* love to do. You remember – all those little wishes, such as taking an art class, a gardening project, learning a language, or _____. (fill in your special wish).

I already hear you saying, "I can't, I don't, I won't." If you love it enough, you can and will make the time to enrich your life. This small step forward will give you the impetus to embrace more of the world around you with your love. Turn your love into active being and don't allow the NAG's resistance to stop you in your path.

We are here to express and experience the very best of ourselves. Here to be the very best that we can be. Why do we put it off? "I'll be better tomorrow," sounds like a Scarlett O'Hara syndrome, right?

Just for today, break out of the box — those rigid lines of living you have imposed on yourself. Live your desires and give yourself permission to do one thing that feels Good to you. (P.S. This isn't a license to go out and have an affair, rob a bank, tell off your boss — none of those really solve your problems.) Trust and act on the love you feel.

It takes courage to follow your heart's desire. It takes trust beyond a wish to allow only Good in your life. We are intimately acquainted with our faults, and when we strive to make changes in our comfortable thoughts of NAG-i-tivity, it can be challenging. Remember, you have great ammunition; all the great qualities you are blessed with come from the Universal Spirit of Good that is your inheritance. Besides, it feels good, and feeling good is worth everything.

Exercise:

- Today, live from the heart.
- Write down what you love.
- Sing what you love.
- Eat what you love.
- Breathe what you love.
- In short, just love. It's a state of mind you are… love.
- It is the key ingredient to every success … love.

This Is the Goodness Experience!

"There is nothing that wastes the body like worry, and one who has any faith in God should be ashamed to worry about anything whatsoever."
— Mahatma Gandhi

GOODNESS NOTES

Be happy.

_____

_____

_____

_____

_____

_____

_____

_____

_____

_____

_____

_____

_____

_____

_____

_____

_____

_____

_____

_____

_____

_____

_____

_____

GOODNESS NOTES

Be calm.

_____

_____

_____

_____

_____

_____

_____

_____

_____

_____

_____

_____

_____

_____

_____

_____

_____

_____

_____

_____

_____

_____

GOODNESS NOTES

Be patient.

_____

_____

_____

_____

_____

_____

_____

_____

_____

_____

_____

_____

_____

_____

_____

_____

_____

_____

_____

_____

_____

_____

WEEK THREE

This is the third week of the Goodness Experience. In the next seven days, you will learn to *accept!* Accept the ideas you have learned and bring them into your life. Live them. Breathe them and experience them.

Acceptance: The final step of knowing, doing and being.

Let's accept all of the wonderful things we are and experience what our lives can be!

DAY 15:   Opening Your Gifts

Your abilities and talents are the gifts you include naturally – gifts to enjoy, experience and treasure every day. You have one-of-a-kind talent no one else possesses. Think about that. You have been groomed, taught and created to express YOU. A gift, a talent—one that is yours and yours alone. These gifts are the key to your heart's desire. Your spiritual heart recognizes your uniqueness of talent, and this allows you to grow endlessly into your own individual fulfillment.

Some of you have never taken the time to cherish these gifts, or have taken them for granted, not seeing that you have something to give everyday that is unique, valuable and worthy. You may not even realize these gifts are anything special or that they even exist. Our talents are buried under the stress of a daily frantic pace and overwhelming burdens in our everyday lives. But with each desire, with its source in Goodness, we have the talent and ability to realize our goal. This is the truth – the love that formed and created the desire will also create its own fulfillment.

One of the most frequent reasons we don't reach our heart's desires is fear brought by the NAG to obscure our hopes. If we don't believe in ourselves, or if we feel a sheer terror of failure, we will stay frozen in a state of wishing we could do this or that. (Remember, MUD and the NAG are the culprits.)

Your Goodness Experience is a journey within yourself, an intimate look at who you are. Not an opinion based on a limited observation, but recognition and complete acceptance of your Goodness identity formed by your Divine Connection.

Remember what talent you felt as you were growing up that you have since set aside and probably forgotten. When I was a kid, I loved to make blueberry muffins for my parents and serve them breakfast in bed. I don't remember if the muffins were good or bad, but the love that was expressed fulfilled my desire to make my parents feel special.

Later, I became too busy with my career and one thousand other distractions. It was easier to order in, pick up or just skip a meal, rather than cook. But, along came instances when I was called upon to cook something. Well, that ability was so hidden in my experience I had convinced myself I must be a disaster in the kitchen. I made excuses and found a way to have someone else cook for me. In the process, my avoiding an ability made me vulnerable to NAG-i-tiv-ity. I had lost my gift of love.

Then came the day when I *had* to cook. The man I was in love with at the time asked me if I could cook. I said, "Of course," and then regretted that declaration immediately. But, my love for him outweighed the fear. I couldn't think of anything more I'd rather do than prepare a meal for his enjoyment. In order for me to overcome my fears, I had to trust through love that I was able to do this. Because of my new understanding of Goodness, I knew if I loved it, I could do it.

His favorite treat was chocolate cake, so that's where I began. I found a recipe for a wonderful chocolate cake and guess what? I made a six layer chocolate cake with warm, go-o-o-o-o-ey chocolate chips in each layer. I did it all from scratch, with love. From this one event, a whole new world opened up to me. I discovered I did, in fact, have the talent I needed. The feeling of inadequacy dissolved. Today I may not be a gourmet cook but I can prepare a beautiful meal for people I love – and you, too, can create a wonderful world of events if you always start with love.

The Goodness Experience is based on love. Regardless of the task – from cleaning house to propelling a vehicle into space at NASA – do it with love, totally, with abandon and freedom, and enjoy this precious commodity which fuels our life.

Even though my chocolate cake experience was a very simple one, this approach can change the direst of problems.

Remember, talent is what you love and lives within your desires.
List 5 talents you have forgotten you possess:

1 _____

2 _____

3 _____

4 _____

5 _____

Make a list of 5 talents you feel are your strongest today:

1 _____

2 _____

3 _____

4 _____

5 _____

Make a list of 5 talents you would like to have:

1 _____

2 _____

3 _____

4 _____

5 _____

Now accept these talents as being a part of your existence. Discover them within yourself. These are your gifts. Today, unwrap at least one of these gifts and remember: love, cherish, and express.

Accomplishment

When you realize your gifts, you will see and experience your Goodness individually and that of the world around you – from your closest family to the most far-reaching point of the world. Like the rippling effect when a pebble is thrown into the water, your energy of Goodness pushes outward from a boundless source and impacts everyone.

GOODNESS NOTES

Every day is a rising star ...

_____

_____

_____

_____

_____

_____

_____

_____

_____

_____

_____

_____

_____

_____

_____

_____

_____

_____

_____

_____

_____

_____

_____

_____

GOODNESS NOTES

Every day is a celebration.

_____

_____

_____

_____

_____

_____

_____

_____

_____

_____

_____

_____

_____

_____

_____

_____

_____

_____

_____

_____

_____

_____

_____

_____

GOODNESS NOTES

Every day is an adventure.

_____

_____

_____

_____

_____

_____

_____

_____

_____

_____

_____

_____

_____

_____

_____

_____

_____

_____

_____

_____

_____

_____

_____

_____

_____

_____

"I'm still in control. It's all your fault."

DAY 16:   Listening – Watching – Knowing

You have the gifts, talents, and abilities to make your desires come to reality, but most of us miss the mark because we don't really know what we want and are unfocused. How many times a day do you think or say, "I don't know what to do / to think / to choose. I'm bored." We sometimes imagine: *If I got that new car / job / hairstyle / dress, that would make me happy.* How many times have you been wrong? I know I have. What are we really looking for?

I have learned we always receive exactly what we need, but we don't always get what we want. That seems unfair, doesn't it? Yet the Universal Laws of Good are always protecting you as well as giving to you in abundance. Until we focus on that Law of Abundance, we are never going to quit chasing goals we can never reach. Now that's frustrating.

You may want to drive a sports car convertible, but you need to test drive your feelings to see if what you want brings you what you desire. *Things* don't bring about feelings; *feelings* bring about things. If you need to know what you really want, ask yourself what you *want* to feel. Since, most of us have quit taking the time to feel, it may take some time to uncover our true feelings. **Listen for the answers.**

Searching for the answer by asking and then listening can get you what you want beyond your wildest imagination.

If you have trouble letting go and listening, the first thing you *must* do is silence the NAG. Yes, she is jumping up and down demanding that brand new car / piece of jewelry / dress / pair of shoes, etc., shouting her mantra: "And who cares about what you feel? These material treasures will solve all your problems, I promise!"

By now you know her game, so open your heart and your mind. Watch. Listen. The answer comes to you when you ask for what you need with an understanding of gratitude, value, beauty, love, and humility. Let go of your preconceived ideas. Take a deep breath. Relax and open your palms upward. Accept what you hear.

Your second step in Listen – Watch – Know is to listen and watch what you are saying in your daily conversations. Are you focused on the positive things you want in your life? Or are you a victim to the NAG, focusing on the NAG-i-tive, tearing down yourself and others? Remember, when you do this, whatever you focus on and talk about is the direction your life will take. When you focus on the weaknesses in yourself or others, emphasizing what's wrong, you'll see this become a reality. Most of the time, we do this unwittingly and, for this reason, we need to be aware and accept only the Good we want in our lives.

Is this another Pollyanna moment? No. In fact, we're exercising our acceptance of what we do want by seeing the Good and positive, and in every moment overcoming the NAG-i-tivity. This does not mean 'grin and bear it,' or 'make the best of it.' It means, if something bad happens or if you're irritated, wanting to find fault, demand to see only Good. This requires you to pause and listen. Good is all there can be – or is! It is your right to see and experience all Good and it moves you along the path of the Goodness Experience.

Give your life, and see what you receive. Now, listen. Accept this as your truth. Your exercise for today is to listen and hear your Divine Connection when you feel in need. Don't just try to fill the hole in your heart and soul, but find the RIGHT answer, the Goodness answer. Watch as the answer unfolds throughout your day. Know that this is the truth.

Accomplishment:

Listening, watching and knowing – essentially living Goodness in every moment – raises the quality of our life, our relationships, our business practices, and our total existence. This power of thinking has the ability to help us to achieve excellence in all of our endeavors.

GOODNESS NOTES

Listen to the message from the wind.

_____

_____

_____

_____

_____

_____

_____

_____

_____

_____

_____

_____

_____

_____

_____

_____

_____

_____

_____

_____

_____

GOODNESS NOTES

Watch Good appear before you.

GOODNESS NOTES

Know that dreams come true.

_____

_____

_____

_____

_____

_____

_____

_____

_____

_____

_____

_____

_____

_____

_____

_____

_____

_____

_____

_____

DAY 17: Freedom

Today's exercise is a discipline to be *free!* Discipline? Free? A contradiction of terms? Not really. Think about what these words mean to you. Go to your heart and ask, "What might freedom be for me?" Listen and apply the meaning to your life. "What does it mean to laugh freely? Live freely? Love freely?" Isn't this a desire that each of you have, regardless of who you are, what you want, or where you are? If you're going to be free, you must realize what is stopping you or causing you to hesitate in the open path to fulfillment.

Make a list of any feelings of limitation you may have. Do you feel not smart enough? Not rich enough? Not pretty enough? Not confident enough? Do you feel you're in a prison with too many things to do, too many responsibilities? These nagging doubts don't come from Goodness. These come from the NAG, so stop them in their tracks today and everyday by understanding your freedom. You're only limited by your thoughts. Banish doubts from your mental kingdom.

Forgiveness is the key to living your freedom. So, if you don't think you're enough in any way, forgive yourself. Forgive yourself and forgive those around you, and appreciate what you do have. This will strengthen and magnify who you are.

Let go of your anger, disappointments and self-pity. Give yourself unconditional love, your most powerful tool for living and loving in the Goodness Experience.

Don't accept anything less than the best from yourself.

List 10 limitations you feel:

1 _____

2 _____

3 _____

4 _____

5 _____

6 _____

7 _____

8 _____

9 _____

10 _____

Everything you have listed as a limitation is solved by seeing the truth of who you are. If it is beauty you want to see, then accept that you possess beauty. Allow beauty to shine from your heart. Look in the mirror and focus on this vibrant quality that express-es our unique-i-city. Your smile can speak a thousand words. Your unfurrowed brow can reveal an openness. Childlike wonder in your eyes can light up a room. See your beauty, expose your beauty. Isn't it about time? Look around your world and watch for beauty everywhere. Your beauty is original, so honor that truth and accept.

List 5 ways to free yourself from your limitations by seeing the op-posite. (Example: "I don't feel rich enough." Use your imagination to treat yourself as though you are the richest person in the world.)

1 _____

2 _____

3 _____

4 _____

5 _____

Whatever you feel you are missing ... *accept* that you always have what you need and *allow* yourself to *experience*. Remember, to *experience* is to see the Good already within you. You have total freedom in what you *accept* and *allow*. In this way, your *action* is power to transform.

If you keep listening to your Divine Connection and *accept* only Good, you will be led to find the answers you need. This is true freedom.

Be free of fear, anxiety, financial problems, hate, anger, resentment, disappointment, self-pity – all the maladies the NAG would love to have you dwell on and ruminate about. It's a waste of time, so get rid of it and *accept* the person you already are.

Accomplishment:

Isn't this the ultimate desire for everyone? Freedom. Breaking barriers we impose on ourselves. When we are finally free of the NAG, we have the ability to soar to our highest expectations and desires. You are now free; it is your birthright.

GOODNESS NOTES

Free for all.

GOODNESS NOTES

I am free.

_____
_____
_____
_____
_____
_____
_____
_____
_____
_____
_____
_____
_____
_____
_____
_____
_____
_____
_____
_____
_____
_____
_____
_____
_____
_____
_____

GOODNESS NOTES

Free to BE.

_____

_____

_____

_____

_____

_____

_____

_____

_____

_____

_____

_____

_____

_____

_____

_____

_____

_____

_____

_____

_____

DAY 18: Do's and Don't's

Today is another exercise of mental discipline.

Each day, we are barraged by the thoughts of what we haven't done, failed to accomplish, unfulfilled desires and a deep-seated yearning for more. We have seen in the past days that we do have everything we need to succeed, even if we forget from time to time. At any moment, we can claim our identity and build from this point of power by focusing on what we *do have* rather than what we *don't have*.

Today as you go through the hours of work, home, or play, close the door and do not let the **Don't's**, the **Can't's** or even the **Won't's** enter. If you hear yourself thinking, "I don't have …," "I don't see how," "I don't know how," or that particularly insidious word **Can't**. Or even worse: "That's not me. I just won't do …," *STOP IT!*

Don't accept NAG-i-tiv-ity for one minute. Don't accept the NAG as anything that even has power. Don't let it find a home in your abundant supply of Goodness thoughts. How in the world could you ever find what you want or need by focusing on what you don't have? Now, that's a NAG-buster.

Now the Do's

- What do you have? ACCEPT only Good – you have everything.
- What do you need? WATCH for Good – you have everything.
- What do you want? EXPERIENCE only Good – you have everything.

Okay, *do* your day.

Accomplishment:

I AM … I CAN … I DO … THE GOODNESS EXPERIENCE!

GOODNESS NOTES

I'm going shopping!

GOODNESS NOTES

I'm going to take a nap.

GOODNESS NOTES

I'm going around the world!

DAY 19:   **Nixing the Nag**

"Ouch. Okay. I'm going. I'm gone."

"Today the NAG is being a real pain. Nothing I do is right. I'm angry, disappointed, intimidated, and sad. So many obstacles that I haven't even attempted to get out from under the covers. I didn't get to sleep until 3 a.m. How did this happen?"

I've heard this from many of my students, including myself. Everything is going great and then the NAG rears her ugly head – AGAIN!

When you have one of these mornings, or afternoons, or evenings, ask yourself the important question: What is true for me today? This question is your protection. What is true for you today is what has been true through each of your discoveries in the Goodness Experience.

The truth is, you may be outgrowing the NAG. We've all been very comfortable for years in the NAG's strangling grip, and she will try to gain you back again. It's up to you to get rid of her for Good. When she surfaces for even a second, let her go. Don't wait for the adrenalin rush – the deceptive thought that maybe she's right. Remember, *do not* give her life.

It's your choice to grow and continue your Goodness Experience. In fact, the NAG's voice is now my warning signal alerting me to what is true and Good about me and my life. I know from experience, if I continue with her on a downward spiral, I'll end up in the M.U.D (Misery, Uncertainty, Doubt).

Use your discipline and strength from all of those positive truths you've learned about your life and your identity, and *choose* to listen to only what is Good and beautiful about you and the world around you. This is not just a silly exercise; it is a conscious reality.

Don't accept that this is going to be a bad day; challenge the NAG as she is on her last leg. Exercise your ability to change the circumstance to Goodness from where you are at this moment.

A Few Reminders ...

1. Acknowledge what you are feeling without making a judgment. Avoid wallowing around in self-pity with the NAG. If you're angry, you can feel it, but don't act on it. Find a solution to neutralize the anger by accepting your Goodness.
2. Acknowledge that there *is* a reason you are feeling this way. But, accept it has no power to control you.
3. Ask yourself, why has it grabbed your attention? Determine if you just go with the flow – or if you will stay in the Goodness Experience.

4. Once you've identified the problem, ask yourself. "What is it I truly want?"

5. Say out loud what you want. Shout it as loud as you can.

6. Affirm that you do have the answer to solve every difficulty, and then listen. If you truly *let go* of the problem and *allow* the answer, your *acceptance* will resolve the problem.

This process is how you listen to what your heart wants and needs. Rather than *react* to the impulse of the NAG, *act* on inspiration. *Reacting* just creates turmoil and confusion, whereas *acting* on inspiration allows you to see the GOODNESS. *Acting* on inspiration rather than impulse is *accepting* your freedom.

Accomplishment:

The nag is nothing more than false fear. Fear is nothing more than 'nag-i-tivity'. Fear and the NAG do not control your life. Goodness does. Let the *unknown* become your adventure.

GOODNESS NOTES

Touch the stars.

GOODNESS NOTES

Fly to the moon.

_____

_____

_____

_____

_____

_____

_____

_____

_____

_____

_____

_____

_____

_____

_____

_____

_____

_____

_____

_____

_____

_____

GOODNESS NOTES

Caress the sun.

DAY 20:   Goodness, Poise and Humility

The Goodness Experience brings balance, continuity, and harmony to your life through your acceptance of humility and poise. As you grow through your day, feel that ease, grace and beauty.

Prior to this, your days were erratic moments of, "Hurry, hurry," and the thread of pressure pounding into your mind. "I don't have enough time. I've got too many responsibilities, too many burdens. I'm mentally famished and need someone to take care of me. I can't see the forest for the trees and just want to quit."

Now you *know* it doesn't have to be this way. You can approach even the most complex task with ease and assurance. The answers you need are with you always. Trust and rely on these powerful tools. As your day unfolds, make it a habit to see the opportunity for Good that presents itself in each moment. As you learn to live from the heart, there is always opportunity available.

One of the worst habits we develop is that of expecting only bad things to happen. It slips into our consciousness like a silent ninja, waiting in full expectancy of catastrophe. We do it unconsciously, and we sabotage our experience. Have you ever been in the midst of a Good feeling and all of a sudden a flash bulletin disrupts your smile? "Oh God, I wonder what terrible thing is going to happen now?" You may not even pay attention to this thought, but it is a culprit, and it sabotages what you are thinking. Better check your self-esteem; maybe you don't feel you deserve Goodness.

The bad habit of expecting the worst to happen can be broken with one thought of humility and poise. That in itself is power. Say, "I will only allow and accept Good into my life." Relax, slowly, gently and lovingly, then listen and watch …

This is Goodness flowing perpetually into your life. It is staying poised within your Goodness Experience, living humility and accepting what is right from your Divine Connection – not what the selfish, self-centered NAG is demanding.

We must accept that Goodness happens 24/7, and *you* are the Goodness Experience. You have been made from Goodness, and the truth of your life is happy and fulfilling. Make your habit one of seeing only Good. This is a spiritual truth, and *spirituality is what we must trust, depend on and rely on.* Stop looking at the material world hoping to see the spiritual progress. Trust the Divine Connection that holds your life in the Goodness Experience.

The miracle is that we have this protection and promise to guide us. No matter your religion or creed, it helps you experience the best of your life.

As your desires grow, so will the challenges. The demand to grow is an ever present law of progress. It moves us to a better understanding and greater fulfillment of ourselves, our lives, and our world. The more you shove your problems under the rug, or see only the obstacle and not the solution, the longer problems will keep you stuck in the MUD. On the other hand, if you focus on the Good in your life, you will see, with ease, a moving grace of Goodness in your heart that is the Goodness Experience.

Accepting the possibility of only Good in yourself is how you see and get to know your highest sense of that incredible person known as you.

The action is simple:

- List the problems facing you today. How does the NAG want you to solve them?
- Now, using poise and humility, what answers do you get from your Divine Connection?

Accomplishment:

Burdens dissolve. Desires find their expression.

GOODNESS NOTES

Pray without ceasing.

_____

_____

_____

_____

_____

_____

_____

_____

_____

_____

_____

_____

_____

_____

_____

_____

_____

_____

_____

_____

_____

_____

_____

GOODNESS NOTES

Play with abandon.

_____

_____

_____

_____

_____

_____

_____

_____

_____

_____

_____

_____

_____

_____

_____

_____

_____

_____

_____

_____

_____

_____

GOODNESS NOTES

Pause in humility.

_____

_____

_____

_____

_____

_____

_____

_____

_____

_____

_____

_____

_____

_____

_____

_____

_____

_____

_____

_____

_____

_____

_____

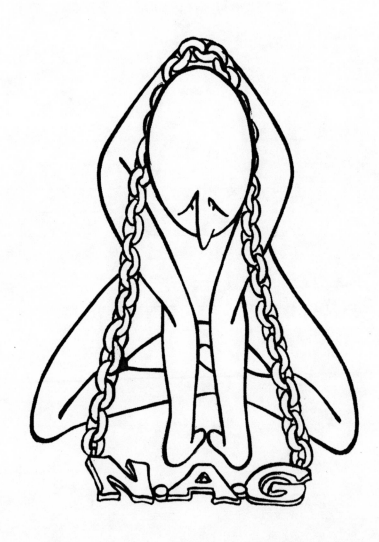

DAY 21:   A Miracle a Day Keeps You on Your Way!

The Goodness Experience defines a miracle as: *transcending the obstacles, rising into a new thought and accepting only what is Good and beautiful about you and your life with absolute certainty.* It's a natural and normal progression – never a freak occurrence. It's like being on a bridge above the turmoil.

Miracles have occurred since Moses parted the Red Sea and Jesus turned water into wine, and healed the blind, the leper, the lame. If we put this into perspective, they transcended the obstacles and saw with certainty the unique Goodness or God in their life.

Material obstacles would try to limit our experience and stop us from seeing the Good we deserve. Once you let go of the obstacles and the limitations, you can see a miracle in every moment. It's a natural and normal way to live with gratitude in every part of your life.

You awaken your miracles with gratitude that leads to confident actions. Make a list of what blessings you have – a friend, a warm cup of coffee, a beautiful rose blooming in the backyard, a windfall of money, finding your soul mate, or finding love in the midst of an argument. Keep making the list until your worries and aggravations dissolve. Recognize that you have everything you need right now; even if you don't see it at the moment. Keep going through your day until all you can feel is warmth and love flowing throughout your being. *Trust.* This is what you deserve.

Begin to count your miracles. List them as they come to you today.

Miracles are always happening around us, but we've been taught they are rare. We don't expect them because we feel unworthy, yet each day is a miracle unto itself. When we focus on seeing these miracles, we see ourselves ascending the barriers and achieving our goal. Take the time to become aware of the miracles that make up your day. Accept and cherish.

If you remain knee deep in worry, anxiety and fear, your MUD will never allow you to even think about a miracle, much less experience one. In the Goodness Experience, your day isn't complete until you have your miracle. Trust that it will come.

List your miracles ...

1 _____

2 _____

3 _____

4 _____

5 _____

Keep going ad infinitum.

Accomplishment:

The Goodness Experience. See Goodness everywhere, for everyone, in everyone.

GRADUATION DAY!

The door is open. Enjoy!

Giving is living the Goodness Experience!

"Can't fight with a graduate of <u>The Goodness Experience</u>."

ABOUT THE AUTHOR

Janice Marie has lived her life applying these 'goodness' principles. An award-winning sales executive with IBM for over 20 years, she used these principles to achieve harmony and success both professionally and personally. A native of Michigan who long resides in Las Vegas, she has hosted a radio show, worked as a motivation speaker, and conducts seminars and workshops globally. She has authored two other books, *Athena: Leadership Skills for the New Millennium* (2000) and *The Gift from the Goddess* (1997).

Happily married for 27 years, the mother of two professional adults and the recipient of a graduate degree from Northwestern University, Janice acknowledges she has spent most of her life studying the power of 'goodness.'

ABOUT THE EDITOR

The Goodness Experience was edited by Jann Robbins. Jann writes, edits, teaches and consults on fiction and non-fiction novels. She co-authored *Hope and Honor*, the non-fiction life story of Major General Sidney , Shachnow and recipient of the Colby Award as Best Book of the year. She also coauthored *In High Places*, a work of fiction with attorney, Phil Taxman. She has recently completed a screenplay, *Never Enough*, based on her husband, Harold Robbins novel of the same title. She currently resides in Los Angeles, California.

A SPECIAL NOTE TO THE READER

Janice Marie is available to conduct workshops, seminars and key note speeches for companies, organizations and special groups. She also has a private coaching practice for those who wish to improve all aspects of their lives. If you are interested in finding out more please contact her at www.thejanicemarie.com

If you would like to bring more Goodness to the world, you can order this book on line at www.thegoodnessexperience.com or send a check or money order to The Goodness Experience 1609 Night Wind Dr. Las Vegas, Nev. 89117 for $19.95 plus $4.00 for shipping and handling. If you have any questions please call 702-233-8305.

Quantity discounts are available upon request.

ORDER FORM

The Goodness Experience   Quantity: _____

AMOUNT ENCLOSED: _____

Send To:

_____

_____

_____

(Please note if you would like the copy signed and to whom)

LaVergne, TN USA
19 August 2010
193892LV00005B/1/A